CANINE
TERMINOLOGY

CANINE TERMINOLOGY

HAROLD R. SPIRA

Illustrated by Mary and Peggy Davidson

The Watermark Press

To Margaret
For all those reasons only she would understand

First published in Australia in 1982
by Harper & Rowe (Australasia).

Reprinted in 2001
by The Watermark Press, Sydney, Australia

National Library of Australia
Cataloguing-in-publication data

Spira, Harold R.
Canine terminology.

ISBN 0949 284 29 7

Dogs – terminology. I Davidson, Marion.
II. Davidson, Margaret. III Title.
636.7'0014

Printed by Kyodo Printing, Singapore

CONTENTS

FOREWORD

This glossary's creation was slow and prolonged; at times, even tedious. Its original concept stems from many years of involvement in the dog world, particularly in the areas of administration, development of breed standards and training of dog judges.

Numerous variations occur in international breed standards terminology; so do some technical inaccuracies. As well, individualistic interpretations add to further misunderstanding.

Existing glossaries and textbooks barely touch the surface of the problem. Most are too brief, incomplete or lack adequate illustrations. Hence this attempt to explain in some detail the many technical and semi-technical phrases and words that abound in the language of dog fanciers.

The research for and actual writing of this book took many months; the usefulness of my work, however, has been immeasurably increased by the drawings accompanying the text. Working with the Davidson twins, Mary and Peggy, must surely rate as one of the happiest experiences in my creative life. The three of us had only just completed a new set of illustrated R.A.S. Kennel Control Breed Standards when publication of this glossary was suggested. Despite the obviously time-consuming aspects of the proposed task, the Davidsons accepted the challenge unhesitatingly. For this I am most grateful, as it is the excellence of their drawings that in my opinion distinguishes this book from other previous attempts in this area.

Mary and Peggy also helped to put the finishing touches to the manuscript, to index it and to proof read it. Really, it is impossible to thank them sufficiently.

Sincere gratitude must also go to my wife Margaret for all her assistance and patience throughout the last two years and, in particular, for the constructive criticism she offered so readily. Without her co-operation and that of the rest of my family, this glossary would not have seen the light of day.

Harold R. Spira
Castle Hill, Sydney

7

PREFACE

Who but a veterinary surgeon, a dog breeder, an international dog judge, a trainer of dog judges and a canine administrator should and could present a book like *Canine Terminology*? Harry Spira is all those things and has done just that. In comparison with other publications touching on the same subject, this book stands out for its clarity of definition and terminology.

The many illustrations and diagrams by the Misses Davidson are a delight, sensitively drawn and perfect in detail.

Presented here is a fund of knowledge that will be of assistance and interest to judges, breeders, exhibitors, veterinary students and all who own and care for dogs. The standard of dogs in Australia is as good as or better than anywhere in the world — as attested to by visiting judges and well-known dog fanciers; now this book will establish a similarly high standard in Australian canine publications. I am sure that it will become the definitive work in this field, not only in Australia, but internationally.

A. Howie President,
Australian National Kennel Council
R.A.S. Kennel Control (New South Wales)

ABBREVIATIONS

A.K.C. American Kennel Club
A.N.K.C. Australian National Kennel Club
F.C.I. Fédération Cynologique Internationale

K.C. Kennel Club (England)
Fig. Figure (illustration) number
syn. Synonym

A

ABDOMEN That part of the body between the chest and the hindquarters. Supported above by the lumbar portion of the spinal column, the abdomen consists of muscular walls and a floor (sometimes referred to as the belly) structured of tough muscular tissue **(Figure 1)**.
See **Figure 55**

Fig. 1 Abdomen, belly and flank

Abdomen, paunchy Loose, flabby abdominal walls, and especially a pendulous underline which, in extreme cases, combine to create a pot-bellied appearance in contrast to a 'tucked-up' abdomen.
See **Figure 356**

Abdomen, tucked-up
See Abdomen, paunchy, Tuck-up

ACETABULUM syn. hip socket, acetabular socket. The relatively deep depression located approximately midway in each half of the pelvic girdle, i.e., at the junction of the ilium, ischium and pubis, into which fits the head of the femur or thigh bone. Together the acetabulum above and the femoral head below form the hip joint. Of varying depths and shapes, according to breed and/or individuals, the acetabulum is closely associated with the disease known as hip dysplasia.
See Hindquarters, Hip dysplasia, **Figures 181, 182, 186a and 186b**

ACHILLES TENDON The longest and strongest tendon in the dog. Easily discernible in short-coated breeds, e.g., Greyhound and Whippet, the Achilles tendon forms an extension of the rear-most thigh muscle groups and provides anchorage for these muscles onto the fibular tarsal bone at the point of the hock **(Figure 2)**.

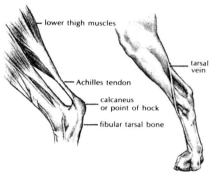

Outward appearance
of Achilles tendon

Fig. 2 Achilles tendon

ACHONDROPLASIA A form of dwarfism primarily affecting the development of long bones, i.e., the limbs, of young dogs. Growth in some areas is restricted or arrested, resulting in an animal normal in head and body development, but severely foreshortened in the limbs. The stunted bones, although lacking in length and frequently bowed, are strong, often stronger than those of normal legs. Dachshunds and Basset Hounds are typical achondroplastics **(Figure 3)**.

It is interesting to note that achondroplasia of genetic origin has been the basis of origin and/or development of a number of dog breeds. Members of the various Dachshund and Basset varieties stand out as examples, in that the rather

Fig. 3 Achondroplasia: Dachshund

short and anatomically deformed limbs, due to achondroplasia, equip them specifically to enter rabbit warrens, badger lairs, etc., a task quite beyond hounds with 'normal' leg formation.
See **Figure 68**

ACROMEGALY A medical terminology for gigantism. The result of abnormal growth patterns involving height, weight, skin and at times also the head, acromegaly is due to pituitary gland influences. Affected animals are well above the 'average' height of 61 cm to 63.5 cm (24 in to 25 in). Their feet are inclined to be large; the skin fits loosely and tends to fold or wrinkle about the head and limbs. Mastiffs with a mass of about 75 kg (165 lb) and measuring from 76.2 cm (30 in) upwards at the withers, serve as good examples of acromegaly **(Figure 4)**.

Acromegalic dogs should not be confused with those known as 'Giant Breeds', some of which achieve even greater heights but are not proportionately as massive.

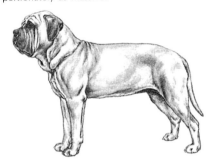

Fig. 4 Acromegaly: Mastiff

ACTION syn. gait, motion, movement. The driving or propelling force in the canine species is the hindquarters, especially the combination of pelvic and upper thigh muscles, assisted by the lower thigh muscle groups. The forequarters, while assisting by providing stabilising and supporting influences, play only a relatively small part in actual propulsion.

The combined efforts of fore- and hindquarters produce the various types of movements referred to in breed standards, e.g., 'smooth powerful rhythmic action' (Dalmatian), 'firm sturdy action' (Chihuahua), 'elastic, swinging, free gait' (Bloodhound), 'long reaching gait' (German Shepherd Dog), 'rolling gait' (Pekingese), etc. The many and varying descriptive adjectives employed clarify (or at least are intended to) the specific types of action required. Most are self-explanatory; those considered unusual are described below.
See Gait

East and west movers Uncommon terminology, used in the A.K.C.'s Schnauzer breed standard, for front feet which are thrown out sideways, away from the centre line.

Free action or **gait** Uninhibited, easy, elastic, strong and untiring movement. A requirement of many breed standards, e.g., Great Dane, Beagle, Dobermann, Siberian Husky, etc.

Hard-driving action Powerful, jerky, rather exaggerated and energy-consuming gait (in contrast to easy, non-tiring movement). Referred to as undesirable in the A.K.C.'s Belgian Sheepdog breed standard.

Mincing action or **gait** Short, choppy, prancing movement, lacking power.

Reachy action Long-striding, untiring and highly economical motion. The opposite to a short-stepping gait.

Rolling action or **gait** Pronounced side-to-side swaying movement typical of barrel-chested, low-legged and/or loosely slung breeds, e.g., British Bulldog, Pekinese. This description may also be applied to the Old English Sheepdog and Pyrenean Mountain Dog, both of which amble.

Rotary motion Specific to the Dobermann breed standard, meaning strong and purposeful gait, coupled with great thrust, thus causing the hocks and stifles to undergo apparently circular or rotary motion when viewed in profile.

Shuffling action Lazy, feet-dragging type of movement, usually considered as undesirable, but requested in the breed standard of the Otter Hound when this animal is walking or moving at a slow trot.

Springy action Bouncing, buoyant and/or elastic motion.

Tottering action or **gait** Swaying, feeble, unsteady gait mentioned as faulty in the A.K.C.'s Boxer breed standard.

Waddling action or **gait** Clumsy, tottering and restricted hindquarters motion due to outwards rotated or bow hocks which, in turn, cause the hind feet to cross when moving past each other.

AITCHES Taken from cattle terminology and interpreted to mean the pelvic tubers. The only reference to 'aitches' occurs in the Sussex Spaniel breed standard when describing the body.
See **Figures 181** and **360**

ALBINISM Congenital non-pigmentation especially affecting the skin, hair and iris coloration.

ALMOND EYES
See Eye Types

ANAL SACS There are two of these, located on each side of the rectum just inside the rim of the anal sphincter. They are sometimes referred to as 'anal glands'. Averaging 1 cm (0.4 in) in diameter, the anal sacs open into the rectal lumen via a short duct. They function as storage chambers for an unpleasant secretion intended partly to coat the stools during the process of defecation. This coating in turn imparts a distinctive odour to the stools, thereby enabling pack animals to trace one another. Blockage of one or other anal gland ducts is not uncommon under domestic circumstances, the major cause being incorrect diet leading to stools that are insufficiently bulky to force sac expression during defecation. Most animals so affected require surgical treatment **(Figure 5)**.

Fig. 5 Position of anal sacs

ANATOMY, COMPARATIVE The bony skeletons of dog and man exhibit remarkable similarity (as indeed do the skeletons of most mammals), the most significant differences being the upright posture adopted by man, the absence of collar bones (clavicles) in the dog, the attachment of the humerus or upper arm of the dog to the chest wall along its entire length (in man it is free), plus the fact that man walks on his whole foot (including the metatarsal bones), whereas the dog walks only on the equivalent of the human toes **(Figure 6)**.

ANATOMY, MUSCULAR Muscles are specialised structures characterised by their power of contraction upon stimulation. According to the microscopic appearance of component muscle fibres, muscles are divided under three headings: striated or skeletal muscles, smooth or visceral muscles and specialised cardiac (heart) muscles. As far as dog judges, breeders, etc., are concerned, the combination of skeletal muscles, especially their upper layers, is important because it plays a major part in creating external (topographical) appearance, as well as being responsible for movement. Muscle development and strength are of particular significance in the forequarters region and in the abdomen/couplings area; in the former area because the forequarters, unlike the hindquarters, are attached to the rib cage by muscles only, and in the latter area as, apart from the spinal column above, there are no bony components **(Figures 7 and 8)**.

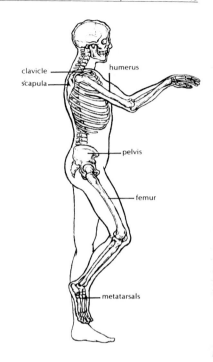

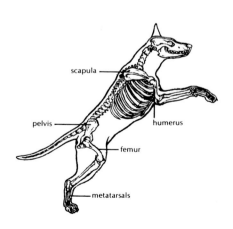

Fig. 6 Comparative anatomy: man and dog

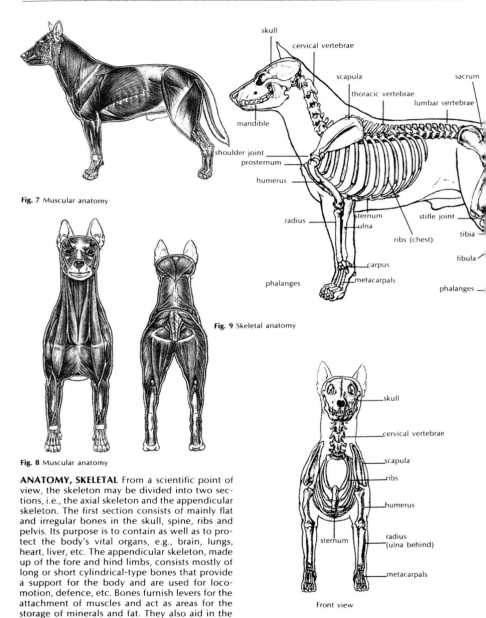

Fig. 7 Muscular anatomy

Fig. 8 Muscular anatomy

Fig. 9 Skeletal anatomy

skull
cervical vertebrae
scapula
thoracic vertebrae
lumbar vertebrae
sacrum
mandible
shoulder joint
prosternum
humerus
radius
sternum
ulna
stifle joint
tibia
ribs (chest)
fibula
carpus
phalanges
metacarpals
phalanges

skull
cervical vertebrae
scapula
ribs
humerus
sternum
radius
(ulna behind)
metacarpals

Front view

Fig. 10 Skeletal anatomy

ANATOMY, SKELETAL From a scientific point of view, the skeleton may be divided into two sections, i.e., the axial skeleton and the appendicular skeleton. The first section consists of mainly flat and irregular bones in the skull, spine, ribs and pelvis. Its purpose is to contain as well as to protect the body's vital organs, e.g., brain, lungs, heart, liver, etc. The appendicular skeleton, made up of the fore and hind limbs, consists mostly of long or short cylindrical-type bones that provide a support for the body and are used for locomotion, defence, etc. Bones furnish levers for the attachment of muscles and act as areas for the storage of minerals and fat. They also aid in the manufacture of blood cells. This book follows

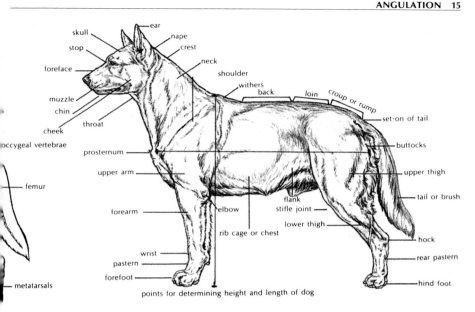

points for determining height and length of dog

Fig. 11 Topographical anatomy

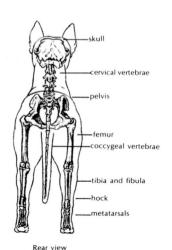

Rear view

the practical course of classifying the skeleton under the headings of head, spine, chest, forequarters and hindquarters **(Figures 9 and 10)**.

ANATOMY, TOPOGRAPHICAL This is concerned with the outward appearance and identification of the various regions of the dog's anatomy **(Figure 11)**.

ANGULATION Probably one of the most frequently used (or misused?) terms amongst dog fanciers, angulation refers to the angles created by bones meeting at various joints (articulations), especially at the shoulder, stifle and hock; the pastern and pelvic areas may also be involved.

In general, the terms 'forequarters angulation' and 'hindquarters angulation' are used to describe the combined joint angles of these regions. Dogs exhibiting a correct range of angulations for a given breed are spoken of as being 'well-angulated' or 'well-turned'. Variations in interpretation of ideal angulation are shown as regards the German Shepherd Dog and the Bouvier des Flandres **(Figures 12 and 13)**.

See **Figure 151** for angulation in relation to gait.

Forequarters angulation With relatively few exceptions (some of which, however, occur in major breeds), the shoulder blade should slope upwards towards the rear at an angle of approximately 90° or more, depending on the

Fig. 12 Angulation: Bouvier des Flandres with ideal angulation

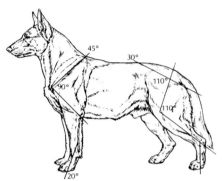

Fig. 13 Angulation: German Shepherd Dog with ideal angulation

breed, with the longitudinal axis of the arm (humerus). This is considered close to anatomical perfection, i.e., the ideal angulation, slope or lay of shoulder, in most breeds, e.g., the German Shepherd Dog **(Figure 14)**.

Hindquarters angulation In line with the forequarters assembly geometry, most standards suggest angles within a range of 90° to 110° for the stifle joint, i.e., the longitudinal axes of the thigh bone (femur) and the lower thigh bone (tibia/fibula). In practice most stifle angulations vary from 110° to 130°, with the Chow Chow as the major variant at 150°. For the hock joint, the term 'angulation' relates to the angle formed by the tibia/fibula combination above and the rear pastern (metatarsals) below. A reference to angulation sometimes also includes the angle formed by the pelvic girdle as related to the spine. This is referred to as the pelvic angle, lay of the pelvis, or pelvic slope **(Figure 15)**.

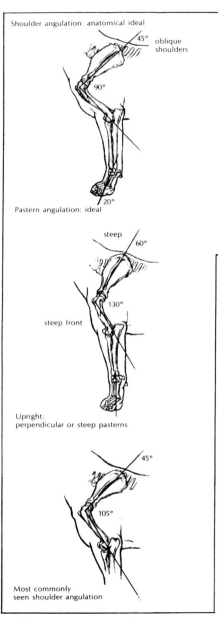

Fig. 14 Shoulder and pastern angulation

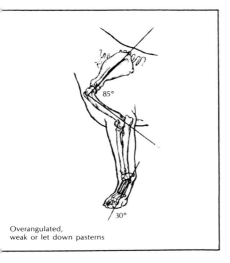

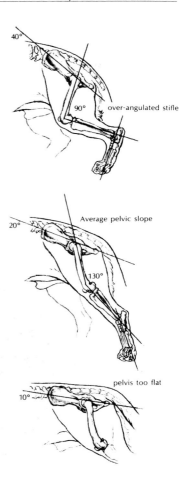

40°

90°   over-angulated stifle

20°   Average pelvic slope

130°

pelvis too flat

10°

Overangulated,
weak or let down pasterns

85°

30°

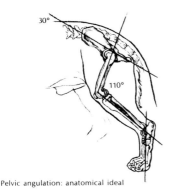

30°

110°

Pelvic angulation: anatomical ideal

Fig. 15 Pelvic, stifle and hock angulation

ANKLE or **ANKLE JOINT** Terminology, adapted from human anatomy, occasionally found in F.C.I. breed standard translations. A synonym for the hock joint.

ANKYLOSIS Firm union or fusion of bones that normally form a movable joint, thus resulting in a stiff joint. Listed as a serious fault in the A.K.C.'s version of the German Shepherd Dog breed standard in relation to the tail.

APEX syn. occiput.

APISH Monkey-like.
See Expression, monkey-like

APPEARANCE, HARD-BITTEN A description peculiar to the Australian Cattle Dog and Australian Terrier breed standards in reference to the rugged and tough outward impression imparted by these breeds.
See **Figure 298**

APPEARANCE, SYMMETRICAL A desired feature of many breeds.
See Balance

APPEARANCE, THOROUGHBRED Resembling a high-quality, aristocratic-looking pure-bred animal in all respects.

APPEARANCE, VARMINTY Used in the West Highland White Terrier breed standard to describe the cheeky, cocky or mischievous look and expression so typical of this breed **(Figure 16)**.

Fig. 16 Varminty appearance: West Highland White

Fig. 17 Apron and frill: Collie (Rough)

APPLE HEAD; APPLE SKULL
See Skull Types

AQUILINE NOSE
See Nose Types

APRON The longish hair under the neck and front section of the chest, typified by the Rough Collie. Basically an extension of the mane into the sides and underneath portion of the neck **(Figure 17)**.

ARCHED LOINS
See Loins

ARCHED NECK
See Neck

ARM The anatomical region between the shoulder and elbow joints, consisting of the humerus and associated muscles. Referred to sometimes as the 'upper arm' in contrast to the 'lower arm', i.e., the section from elbow to wrist **(Figure 18)**.
See Forequarters, Angulation

Fig. 18 Arm: upper arm, forearm and elbow

ARTICULATE; ARTICULATION The union of two or more bones to form a joint, e.g., 'the kneecap (patella) articulates with the lower end of the thigh bone (femur) within the confines of the stifle joint', or 'the articulation of shoulder blade (scapula) and arm (humerus) creates the shoulder joint'.
See Forequarters, Shoulder joint, **Figure 137**, Stifle, **Figure 305**, Angulation, **Figures 14** and **15**

ARTIFICIAL INSEMINATION The deposition of male spermatozoa into a bitch's genital tract by artificial means; an often practised technique in the canine species to obtain fertilisation when normal coitus, for one reason or another, is not possible.

B

BACK In anatomical terms, the back is that portion of the topline commencing from a point just behind the withers and ending at the loins/croup junction, i.e., the combined thoracic and lumbar vertebral regions of the spine. (*See* **Figures 11** and **300**) It appears generally accepted that, for purposes of normal physiological function, a dog's back should be (a) relatively broad and well-muscled, especially over the loins or coupling area, where such muscling tends to form a rise, (b) approximately level, i.e., equidistant in height from withers to ground and loins to ground, or slope downwards gently from the withers to the croup and (c) in length should slightly exceed shoulder height by a ratio of about 10:9. Whilst the majority of breed standards indeed call for backs fitting within these parameters, many more specific and/or individualistic requirements are requested in some. Examples include long, short, roach, soft, etc. *See* Back Types

BACK TYPES

Back arched over the loins Almost self-explanatory, this description is usually applied to straight or level backs that exhibit an arch, varying in degree or extent over the loins area. In most cases such rise is due entirely to muscle development and denotes desirable strength in that area. Examples of breed standards requesting such construction include Bull Terrier, Dachshund, Rhodesian Ridgeback, etc. **(Figure 19)**.

Fig. 19 Arched loins: rise over loins

Back dropping through withers A backline similar in some respects to a hollow back, but affecting only the front section immediately behind the withers. Considered as faulty construction, such a back is due to looseness of shoulder muscles rather than to actual spinal weakness **(Figure 20)**.

Fig. 20 Carp or camel back

Camel back syn. hump or humped back. A form of roached back, first dipping behind the shoulders then arching markedly in front of and over the loins before once again dropping at the rump. The degrees of arch and/or dip may vary appreciably **(Figure 21)**.

Fig. 21 Drop through withers: dip (nick) behind shoulders

Carp back Another kind of roach back, similar to a camel back except that there is little or no initial drop behind the shoulders, and the arch tends to be not as high **(Figure 21)**.

Dip or **Dippy back** syn. hollow back.

Flat back syn. table top back. A back which is both horizontal, i.e., the same distance from the ground at the shoulders and over the loins, as well as straight, without dip or rise along its entire length **(Figure 22)**.

Fig. 22 Flat withers: flat or level back

Hollow back syn. dipped or dippy back, saddle back, slack back, soft back, swampy back, sway back. A back that sags or is concave to some degree along its entire length. The actual extent of sag may vary in depth, position and/or distance involved **(Figure 23)**.

Fig. 23 Hollow, dippy, sway, swamp, soft or weak back

Horizontal back
See Flat back

Hump or **Humped back** syn. camel back.

Level back One in which the height at the withers is identical to that over the loins, yet one that is not necessarily straight or flat **(Figure 22)**.

Long back One in which the distance from the withers to the rump appreciably exceeds the height at the withers, or one in excess of the length required by the breed standard **(Figure 24)**.

Fig. 24 Long back

Overbuilt back The result of excessive muscle development over the rump area, giving a padded, overbuilt appearance, with or without rise in backline towards the rear **(Figure 25)**.

Fig. 25 Overbuilt rump

Roach or **Roached back** By strict definition, a roach back is one that is arched or convex to some degree and/or extent. Slightly different forms are known as camel, carp or wheel backs.

A simple roached back is one that is arched or roached to some degree along its length, but does not include the loin area **(Figure 26)**. When the roach includes the loin area it is known as a camel or carp back. If it extends along the whole of the back region right to the tail root, it is more correctly referred to as a wheel back.

Although in most instances considered to be a faulty construction, a roach back is required by some breed standards, e.g., Manchester Terrier ('slight roach'). When judging, it is essential to distinguish between a true roach, i.e., caused by vertebral contour of the spine and a slightly roached appearance produced by muscular development over the loin area. The latter, if not too exaggerated, is a sign of strength and is requested in numerous breed standards.
See Back arched over the loins

Fig. 26 Roached back

Saddle back syn. hollow back.

Short back Either a back shorter than height at withers or one merely short in relation to specific breed requirements. A Dachshund, for example, may be 'short in back' for this variety in spite of being considerably longer than its height **(Figure 27)**.

Fig. 27 Short, straight back

Slack back or **Slackness of back** A mild form of hollow or sway back, due to structural weakness of one form or another, e.g., undue length (especially in relation to height), inadequate muscular support, loose ligamentation, senility, repeated pregnancies, etc. In the Wire Fox Terrier breed standard, for example, slackness of back is listed as a fault, as applied both to a dip in the back immediately behind the withers as well as to an excess of space between the back ribs and the hip bones **(Figure 23)**.

Sloping back Normally taken as one in which the height, measured at the withers, exceeds that over the loins, i.e., a back sloping downwards to

Fig. 28 Sloping back: high in withers

the rear **(Figure 28)**. Such construction is demanded in numerous breed standards, e.g., Dobermann, Alaskan Malamute, etc. However, a slope in the opposite direction, i.e., from higher loins down towards the withers, is also in the realms of possibility, e.g., Old English Sheepdog and Chesapeake Bay Retriever; in these breeds such a slope is considered desirable **(Figure 29)**.

Fig. 29 Back sloping to front or rising to rear, low in withers

Soft back A mild form of hollow back; one showing only a slight tendency to sag or bend **(Figure 23)**.

Straight back One that runs in a straight line, without dip or arch from withers to loin, e.g., English Toy Terrier. Such a backline need not necessarily be level; it can, in fact, slope either way **(Figure 27)**.

Swampy back syn. hollow back.

Sway back syn. hollow back.

Table top back syn. flat back.

Wheel back A form of roach back which is more exaggerated in curve than a carp or camel back, and runs in a continuous arch from withers to tail, e.g., Bedlington Terrier, Borzoi **(Figure 30)**.

Fig. 30 Wheel back

Backbone syn. spinal column.
See Anatomy, skeletal

Backline That portion of the entire topline of a dog, beginning at the rear end of the withers and ending at the tail **(Figure 31)**.

Fig. 31 Topline and backline

Back skull
See Skull

BADGER syn. beaver, blaireau, hare, jasper. Basically an admixture of white/grey/brown/black hairs of varying intensity, badger is a not uncommon coat colour of dogs, especially in a variety of Hound breeds, e.g., Basset Griffon Vendeen (badger-pied), Artois Hound (hare or badger patches), Pyrenean Mountain Dog (badger or blaireau markings). In most such breeds badger colouring occurs in patches about the head and/or body, placed on a basic white background. Such specimens are termed 'badger pied' **(Figure 32)**.
See Pied

Fig. 32 Badger colouring: Pyrenean Mountain Dog

BADGER PIED
See Badger and Pied

BALANCE syn. symmetry, symmetrical appearance. A descriptive noun frequently employed by dog breeders, exhibitors, and especially judges to describe the pleasing, harmonious and well-proportioned blend-in of an animal's parts and features, resulting in a final, composite effect of total symmetry: the aim of all connoisseurs of the canine race.

The verb 'to balance' is used to explain the relationship of one anatomical area to another, e.g., 'tail to balance body' (Cavalier King Charles Spaniel) suggesting a tail length, achieved by docking, to complement body proportions. 'Balanced' is frequently applied to skull components, i.e., equal lengths of brain case in relation to foreface, e.g., Afghan Hound breed standard (A.K.C.).

BANDY A reference to outward bowed fore or hind legs.
See Legs, bandy, Gait, **Figure 152**, Front Types, **Figure 144**, Rear views, **Figure 272**

BAR syn. arm or humerus.

BARREL; BARRELLED
See Ribs, barrel

BARREL CHEST
See Ribs, Chest capacity

BARRELLED VENT
See Vent, barrelled

BAT EARS
See Ear Types

BEADY EYES
See Eye Types

BEARD The arrangement of thick, longish and stand-offish hair, often of wiry texture, around the chin, cheeks, sides of face and lower jaw regions of some breeds. The extent, distribution, length and texture of beard hair has great influence on the facial characteristics and expression of numerous breeds, e.g., Wire-haired Dachshund, Bearded Collie, Griffon Bruxellois, Bouvier des Flandres, Afghan Hound, etc. **(Figure 33)**.
See Whiskers, **Figures 107, 140, 221 and 353**

BEAUTY SPOT A distinct, round patch of coloured hair, ideally situated in the centre of a white blaze on the topskull between the ears. Whilst the term 'beauty spot' appears to be applicable to most breeds, 'spot' or 'lozenge mark', referring to similar markings in the Cavalier King Charles and King Charles Spaniels are specific to these two breeds respectively **(Figure 34)**.
See **Figure 212**

Fig. 33 Beard, bushy eyebrows, whiskers and moustache: Wire-haired Dachshund

Fig. 34 Beauty spot, kissing spot or lozenge mark

BEAVER
See Badger

BEEFY A colloquialism to describe an over-conditioned, muscular animal, i.e., a dog carrying excessive poundage, usually referring to meat or muscle rather than fat.

BEE-STING TAIL
See Tail Types

BELLY The underpart, underline or muscular floor of the abdomen.
See **Figures 1** and **278**

BELTON A specific colour pattern found in the English Setter. The word 'Belton' (the name of a village in Northumberland) was used by Edward Laverack, considered to be the founder of the English Setter as it is today, in his book written in 1875, to describe the ticking or roan coat colour patterns, either light or dark, in this breed. Several such colours are recognised: blue belton (black and white), orange belton (orange and white), lemon belton (lemon and white), liver belton (liver and white) and tricolour (blue belton with tan patches under eyes) **(Figure 35)**.

Fig. 35 Belton: English Setter

BI-COLOUR By definition, composed of two colours. Used in Hound breeds to describe a coat of two colours, the basic one of which is white, e.g., Basset Griffon Vendeen. In other breeds, e.g., German Shepherd Dog and Dobermann, more specifically employed for a basically black dog with restricted tan points on head, legs and chest, or a blue and liver dog with similar tan markings (Bedlington Terrier, A.K.C. breed standard) **(Figure 36)**.
See **Figure 266**

Fig. 36 Bi-colour or Skewbald: Harrier

BI-LATERAL CRYPTORCHID
See Cryptorchid

BIRD OF PREY EYES
See Eye Colour

BITCH A female of the canine species.

BITE The name given to the position of the upper and lower teeth in relation to each other when the mouth is closed. The types of bite described in the breed standards are numerous.

Irregular bite A bite in which one, some, or occasionally all incisors, either upper or lower, have erupted in abnormal fashion. Numerous vari-

ations and gradations from normal can, and in fact do, occur in the area of bites. Generally speaking, most judges show reasonable tolerance towards minor imperfections, but penalise heavily in severe cases. The often-expressed view that jaw development, strength and dimensions, e.g., length, width, composition and depth of bone are probably of greater importance than actual incisorial alignment unquestionably has a great deal to recommend it.

Level bite Some confusion exists in the interpretation of this type of bite. Many experts hold it to be synonymous with a pincer bite. Yet some breed standards define it as being different, e.g., the American Staffordshire Terrier, according to its breed standard, is required to have a level mouth and a reverse scissors bite. In all probability, the term 'level bite' is intended to refer to upper and lower jaws of equal length, i.e., level, rather than actual teeth positions.
See Mouth, level, **Figure 222**

Overshot bite A receding, often weakly constructed lower jaw. In this form of bite the lower incisors are situated some distance behind their upper counterparts; hence no physical contact takes place between their outer surfaces and the inner ones of the upper incisors. Other names used to describe this condition are parrot-jawed, pig-jawed, shark mouth and swine mouth **(Figure 37)**.

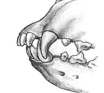

Fig. 37 Overshot bite: pig jaw

Pincer bite syn. vise-like bite. One in which the horizontal or cutting surfaces of the upper and lower incisor teeth meet edge to edge when the mouth is shut; according to the breed standards, such bites are permitted in the Airedale Terrier, West Highland White Terrier, Mastiff, etc. **(Figure 38)**.

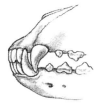

Fig. 38 Pincer or level bite

Scissors bite By far the most common arrangement, this is defined as one in which the outer surfaces of the lower incisor teeth engage with the inner surfaces of the upper incisors when the mouth is shut. For absolute perfection, the teeth forming a scissor bite should erupt at approximately 90° angles (i.e., be set square) from jaws of equal length (i.e., level jaws or level mouth). They should be strong and of normal size, evenly positioned and uncrowded in their arrangement within the dental arches, plus have their cutting edges in horizontal alignment **(Figure 39)**.

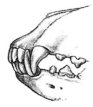

Fig. 39 Scissors bite

Scissors bite, reverse One in which the lower jaw is somewhat longer than the upper one, causing the lower incisors to be positioned slightly in front of their upper counterparts. This results in the inner surfaces of the lower incisors engaging in direct contact with the outer surfaces of the upper ones when the mouth is closed, e.g., Mastiff, American Staffordshire Terrier breed standards.

Undershot bite An under jaw appreciably longer than the upper one and frequently turned up as well, e.g., British Bulldog, resulting in a bite in which the lower incisors erupt well in front of those in the upper jaw. No physical contact occurs between upper and lower incisor teeth in such a mouth **(Figure 40)**.
See **Figure 57**

Fig. 40 Undershot bite

BLADE-BONE, BLADE or **BLADES** syn. shoulder blade or scapula.

BLAIREAU
See Badger

BLANKET; BLANKET MARKINGS Large areas of colour extending over the back and sides, and occasionally up the neck as well. A term frequently used when describing Hound markings **(Figure 41)**.
See Mantle

Fig. 41 Mantle or blanket: Levesque

BLAZE A rather broad and fairly extensive white marking (smaller and narrower types are called 'stars' and 'stripes' respectively), starting near the top of the skull region and running down the forehead to the muzzle. A common occurrence in many breeds, e.g., Beagle, Boston Terrier. Also occasionally used to describe a similar type of marking on the chest, e.g., Airedale Terrier (A.K.C. breed standard) **(Figure 42)**.
See **Figures 159, 264** and **304**

Fig. 42 Blaze: Pyrenean Mountain Dog

BLOCKY Meaning solid or squarish, used to describe excessive width in relation to length, especially as applied to head properties. A blocky head, for example, is one that is broader and coarser than ideal **(Figure 43)**.

Fig. 43 Normal head proportions (left), contrast to blocky (right)

BLOOM The outward appearance, especially as related to coat properties, of good health and well-being. Generally taken as high quality, lustrous, glossy and well-distributed coat.

BLUE A dilution of black coat colour, due to a recessive gene influence. Either light or dark blue-grey in appearance, this colour is a normal occurrence in a number of breeds, e.g., Kerry Blue Terrier, Bedlington Terrier, etc. However, it is considered undesirable in many others, in which it is usually associated with general pigmentary dilution, and, especially light eye colour, e.g., German Shepherd Dog.

BLUE BELTON
See Belton

BLUE MERLE
See Merle

BLOWN COAT
See Coat

BOBBED TAIL
See Tail Types

BOBTAIL An alternative name for the Old English Sheepdog. Also refers to a tail which has been docked to an extremely short length, or to a dog born tailless, e.g., Schipperke **(Figure 44)**.

BODY The anatomical section between the fore- and hindquarters. It consists of the chest in front and the abdomen at the rear. The body's upper portion is made up of the thoracic and lumbar sections of the spine. Below, it is enclosed by the sternum and muscular abdominal floor. The chest is separated from the abdomen by a tough elastic musculo-tendinous sheet called the diaphragm.
See **Figure 11**

Body, deep through the heart An unusual expression, meaning good depth of chest, e.g., Golden Retriever breed standard.

Fig. 44 Bobtail: Old English Sheepdog

Body length Unless otherwise specified in the breed standard, the body length of an animal is taken as the distance from the point of the shoulder to the rearmost projection of the upper thigh (or point of the buttocks).
See **Figure 216**

Body, loosely slung Construction in which the attachment of the body at the shoulders and/or pelvis is looser than desirable. Usually due to weak ligament construction. Animals so constructed frequently exhibit an abnormal degree of looseness or wobble when gaiting.

BODY SPOTS Patches of colour, usually black, on the skin, but not on the coat of dogs. A common and acceptable feature in numerous breeds, e.g., Bull Terrier, (White), Fox Terrier and many Hounds.

BONE A reference taken to be synonymous with substance and relating in particular to thickness, quality and strength of bone, especially as measured in the forearm region. The Foxhound breed standard serves as a good example, asking for 'the legs to be full of bone right down to the feet, and not tapering off in any way'. The suggestion here is for strong, clean bone, almost identical in circumference (i.e., cylindrical in shape) from elbow to feet.

The range of words used to describe bone in the canine species is vast. The desirable terminology includes the words: correct amount, adequate, substantial, strong, ample, and medium. At either end lie: coarse, loaded and heavy, contrasted by fine, weak, insufficient, spindly, hyper-refined and delicate. There are others **(Figure 45)**.

Bone, good composition Used in the German Short-haired Pointer breed standard to describe clean, healthy, sound, and strong bone, i.e., the opposite to porous bone and/or clumsy bone.

Bone shape A reference to shape of bone in cross-section (as taken through the forearm).

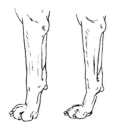

Fig. 45 Heavy bone (left) and light bone (right)

Three basic forms are mentioned in the breed standards. These are flat bone, e.g., Gordon Setter; oval bone, e.g., Pointer and Belgian Malinois and round bone, e.g., Dobermann.

Bone, sound Properly structured bone of correct chemical composition, shape, strength and density, devoid of bumps, lumps or any signs of weakness and deformity.

BOSSY, BOSSY IN SHOULDERS
See Shoulders, loaded

BOUNCE Movement characterised by a greater degree of buoyancy, elasticity and springiness than usual.

BOW HOCKS
See Hocks

BRACELETS The name given to the unshaven areas of hair on the hind legs of Poodles prepared in the Continental clip.
See **Figures 267** and **277**

BRAIN ROOM, PLENTY OF Unusual terminology employed by some breed standards, e.g., English Setter, Irish Setter, ensuring adequate skull width, especially in relation to length. A colloquialism based on the incorrect assumption that skull dimensions exert great bearing upon intelligence.

BRACHYCEPHALIC
See Skull Types

BREAK Used both as a verb and as a noun (a) to describe coat colour changes. In the Bearded Collie, for example, puppies born black/white begin to 'break' into their adult slate-grey at about three to four months of age. Similar colour changes occur in the Australian Terrier, Kerry Blue Terrier, etc. and (b) related to stop development. Cocker Spaniel breeders, for example, speak of puppies' heads beginning to 'break' during the process of topskull and foreface plane separation, coupled with stop formation. This process normally begins at four to six months of age; (c) as a noun, 'break' refers to the crease line in the ear lobe, i.e., the line of demarcation or fold separating the upright and dropped portion of an ear, e.g., Rough Collie, Fox Terrier.
See Ears, Break of

BREASTBONE syn. sternum.
See Chest Anatomy

BREECH As in 'breech musculation' referred to in the Boxer standard. The area designated by the inner thigh muscle groups around the buttocks.
See **Figures 8, 46b** and **307**

BREECHES; BREECHING syn. culottes, pants, trousering, trousers. This has three meanings: (a) fringing of longish hair at the posterior borders of the upper and, at times, lower thigh regions, e.g., English Setter, Keeshond **(Figure 46a)**. (b) The ridge-like pattern of longer than usual hair in short-coated breeds at the junction of inner and outer thighs, e.g., Dobermann **(Figure 46b)**. (c) More specifically, in the Manchester Terrier, the tan-coloured hair on the outside of the hind legs.
See **Figures 35** and **61**

Fig. 46a Breeches, pants, trousers or culottes

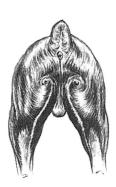

Fig. 46b Breeches on short-coated dog

BREEDS, CLASSIFICATION OF Dogs, generally speaking, are divided into groups according to usage. Whilst the American Kennel Club (A.K.C.) and Kennel Club (England), and therefore also the Australian governing bodies, employ six groups, the Fédération Cynologique Internationale (F.C.I.) uses four principal categories, usually divided into ten sub-groups.

Basically, Hounds and Gundogs are those bred essentially for hunting purposes. Working Dogs find employment in herding, hauling or guarding, as well as many other tasks beneficial to man. Terriers often were, and still are, engaged by huntsmen to aid Hounds in seeking out prey from burrows, for ratting and fighting (now officially banned in most countries), etc. Toy breeds are considered as pets only, whilst the Non-Sporting group consists of a mixture of breeds mostly without specific purpose, but which, for technical reasons, do not fit readily into other groups. The F.C.I. includes the Terriers in its Hunting Dogs classification, together with Hounds and Gundogs, and lists a separate category for Greyhound breeds.

BREEDS, GIANT
See Giant Breeds

BREED STANDARDS The set of breed descriptions originally laid down by the various parent breed clubs and nowadays accepted officially by the international bodies, namely the K.C. (Kennel Club of England), A.K.C. (American Kennel Club) and F.C.I. (Fédération Cynologique Internationale). At the time of writing, the Australian National Kennel Control and its supporting state organisations recognise and use the breed standards laid down by the English Kennel Club.

BRICK-SHAPED HEAD
See Head Types

BRINDLE; BRINDLING A colour pattern produced by the presence of darker hairs forming bands and giving a striped effect on a background of tan, brown or yellow. Brindle occurs in many breeds, e.g., Great Dane, Boston Terrier, Irish Wolfhound, Scottish Terrier, etc. The extent of brindling may vary greatly, according to the intensity of individual hair pigmentation as well as with the extent of stripe distribution. Some brindle specimens, e.g., Boston Terriers, might appear almost black at first sight, whereas in others brindling may be of rather light intensity, e.g. Irish Wolfhound, Cairn Terrier **(Figure 47)**.

BRISKET Mostly taken as a synonym for breastbone or sternum. In some breed standards (e.g., British Bulldog, which reads 'the brisket should be capacious'), it is used in place of chest or thorax.
See Chest anatomy, Sternum

Fig. 47 Brindle: Greyhound

Deep brisket; deep in brisket syn. well-developed brisket, well let down brisket, deep chest, deep in chest, deep in ribs. A reference to a chest well-developed in depth, i.e., normally one in which the brisket reaches down at least to the elbow region; the opposite to a shallow chest. The term is another way of expressing adequate chest depth, e.g., breed standards of Bichon Frisé, American Water Spaniel, Borzoi, etc. **(Figure 48)**.
See Chest, Deep in

Fig. 48 Deep brisket or chest

Good depth brisket
See Deep brisket

Shallow brisket
See Deep brisket, Chest, Depth of

Well-developed brisket
See Deep brisket, Chest, Depth of

Well let down brisket
See Deep brisket

BRISTLE COAT
See Coat

BROKEN COAT
See Coat

BROKEN COLOUR
See Colour, Broken

BROKEN-UP-FACE
See Face, Broken-up

BROWS syn. superciliary arches or ridges. The ridges formed above the eyes by frontal bone contours. Part of the forehead, brows, vary in type and prominence according to the breed, e.g., Beagle **(Figure 49a)**. For instance, they are required to be 'very prominent' (British Bulldog), 'somewhat prominent' (Saint Bernard). At the op-

Fig. 49a Brows and blunt muzzle: Beagle

Fig. 49b Overhanging brows: Clumber Spaniel. Note vine-shaped ears

posite end of the scale, the A.K.C.'s Rough Collie breed standard requests 'very slight prominence of eyebrows'. Factors other than mere bone structure influence brow appearance, e.g., coat growth and trimming in the Schnauzer, Scottish Terrier and Bouvier des Flandres, give rise to 'bushy' eyebrows, or the relatively loose amount of skin over the eyebrows in the Sussex Spaniel and Chow Chow impart a 'frowning' expression **(Figure 49b)**.
See **Figures 103, 110** and **114**

BROWN NOSE
See Nose Types

BRUSH (a) A synonym for tail, especially one which is covered in bushy, medium-length, full-furred hair (see **Figure 309**) (b) the fox-like, relatively short-furred hair covering some tails, e.g., Siberian Husky (c) Fore or hind legs that move so close to one another that they touch or brush at their inner borders, e.g., brushing fore and/or aft is an abnormal form of movement (see **Figure 152**).

BRUSHED TAIL
See Brush, Tail Types

BULGING EYES
See Eye Types

BULGING CHEEKS
See Cheeks

BURR An irregular, bump-like, cartilagenous formation on the inside of the external ear canal. Mentioned in the description of a British Bulldog's rose ear, i.e., 'showing part of the inside of the burr'.
See **Figures 81, 101b** and **212**

BUTTERFLY NOSE
See Nose Types

BUTTOCKS The muscular area surrounding the ischiatic tubers of the pelvis. Above, the buttocks merge into the croup, whilst below they blend with the upper thigh region.
See Hindquarters, **Figures 11 and 307**

BUTTON EARS
See Ear Types

C

CABRIOLE FRONT
See Front Types

CALCANEUS The uppermost extension of the large fibular tarsal bone in the hock joint. In topographical terms, the so-called 'point of the hock', it serves as an anchorage area for the Achilles tendon.
See Hindquarters, **Figures 2, 181** and **187**

CAMEL BACK
See Back Types

CANDLE FLAME EARS
See Ear Types

CANINES; CANINE TEETH
See Dentition

CANKER Colloquialism for a specific infection of the external ear canal. Technically known as *otitis externa*, canker is a relatively common ailment in the dog, particularly in drop-eared breeds. Size and shape of the lumen, ventilation, aeration, hair growth inside the canal, exposure to wind, water, dust and pollen, etc., may act as predisposing agents.

CANNON; CANNON BONE Rare term borrowed from horse terminology, synonymous with the pastern or metacarpus and used in the Brittany Spaniel standard.

CANTER
See Gait

CANTHUS
See Eye Anatomy

CAP Darkly shaded colour pattern on the skull of some breeds, extending downwards to the eyes. Also referred to as a 'widow's peak'. Examples include the Siberian Husky and Alaskan Malamute **(Figure 50)**.
See Figure 215

CAPE Profuse, often harsh hair, enveloping the shoulder region of some breeds, e.g., Schipperke, Old English Sheepdog. Virtually an extension of the neck ruff.
See **Figures 44** and **218**

CARNASSIAL TEETH The name given to the last or fourth premolars in the lower jaw, as well as

Fig. 50 Cap: Siberian Husky

Fig. 51 Carnassial teeth: lower first molar (left), upper fourth premolar (right)

the first molars in the upper jaw **(Figure 51)**.
See Dentition

CARP BACK
See Back Types

CARPAL JOINT syn. carpus, wrist. The joint between the forearm and the pastern on the front leg.
See Forequarters

CARROT TAIL
See Tail Types

CAT FOOT
See Feet Types

CAUDAL VERTEBRAE syn. coccygeal vertebrae. The tail vertebrae.
See Spinal column, **Figure 300**

CHARACTER Used in reference to temperament. Dogs, mentally equipped to perform those functions for which they were designed originally, are referred to as being 'true in character' for that particular breed.

CHEEK or **CHEEKS** The fleshy regions at the sides of the head, commencing at the lip junction, and extending backwards into the masseter muscles area, a little below the eyes.
See **Figure 11**

Bulging cheeks; bulging in cheeks
See Cheeky

Clean in cheeks Dogs structurally lean and/or unexaggerated in this area, i.e., without decided cheek muscle bulges, are often referred to as being 'clean in cheeks' **(Figure 52)**.

Fig. 52 Clean in cheeks, chiselling : Fox Terrier

Coarse in cheeks
See Cheeky

Fleshy in cheeks Refers to a greater degree of cheek muscle development than ideal. Similar to, but not as marked as, coarse cheeks, i.e., the opposite to lean cheeks **(Figure 53)**.

Fig. 53 Cheeky, clown face: Staffordshire Bull Terrier

Lean in cheeks syn. clean cheeks. Cheeks only lightly covered with muscle. A requirement of some Toy breed standards, e.g., Chihuahua **(Figure 52)**.

CHEEK BUMPS Bulging or prominent cheek areas caused by incorrect bone formation, excessive muscle development or a combination of both. Mentioned as a fault in the Saint Bernard breed standard.
See **Figure 252**

CHEEKY syn. bulging in cheeks, cheekiness,

fleshy in cheeks, coarse in cheeks. Dogs with bulging, bumpy or over-developed cheek muscles, at times in concert with coarse bone, are frequently described as 'cheeky', 'fleshy in cheeks', 'coarse in cheeks' or as exhibiting signs of 'cheekiness'. The Staffordshire Bull Terrier serves as a good example of maximum cheek development: in this breed, it is a desirable feature **(Figure 53)**.

CHERRY NOSE
See Nose Types

CHEST syn. brisket, thorax. That section of the body between the neck in front and the abdomen behind.
See **Figure 11**

Chest anatomy Situated between the neck and abdomen, the chest is composed of thirteen thoracic vertebrae above, thirteen ribs on each side and the sternum below. The sternum (syn. breastbone or brisket) consists of a row of eight individual bones or sternebrae joined by blocks of cartilage. Between them, these form the floor of the thorax or chest. The first sternebra, the manubrium, is the longest. That part of the manubrium positioned ahead of the shoulder joint when seen in profile and situated centrally between the two shoulder blades is termed the 'prosternum' or 'point of the breastbone'. The last sternebra is known as the xiphoid process.

The ribs articulate directly with the sides of the thirteen thoracic vertebrae above. Below, the arrangement is more complicated. The first eight ribs join their respective sternebrae by means of individual costal or rib cartilages. The ninth rib links into the costal cartilage of the eighth rib. The tenth, eleventh and twelfth ribs in turn hinge into the lower section of the ninth rib. The thirteenth rib, the shortest of all, remains entirely unattached below. In line with their mode of attachment, the first nine ribs are known as 'true' ribs, the tenth, eleventh and twelfth ribs as 'false' ribs, whilst the thirteenth is called the 'floating' rib. In front, the chest extends into the neck. At the rear, it blends into the abdomen, from which it is separated by the diaphragm **(Figure 54)**.
See Anatomy, skeletal, **Figures 9** and **10**

CHEST CAPACITY Composed externally of the thoracic vertebrae above, the ribs on the sides and the sternum below, the chest contains and protects a number of vital organs, such as the heart, lungs, etc. As optimum development of these organs is linked directly to health, exercise tolerance and performance, it follows that chest capacity is of major importance **(Figure 55)**.

A dog's chest is measured in three dimensions: depth, length and width. For superior stamina, a desirable feature according to most breed standards, all these measurements should be optimal

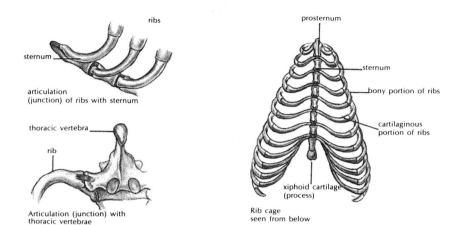

Fig. 54 Ribs or chest anatomy

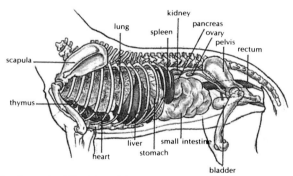

Fig. 55 Viscera: position of organs in relation to bony skeleton

within the stated parameters, to give maximum chest capacity for that particular breed.

Apart from differences in width, depth and length, the chests of dogs also exhibit variations in shape. This is related directly to rib contours. In some breeds, e.g., British Bulldog, rounded or well-arched ribs are called for; these impart a 'barrelled' or 'barrel-chested' appearance. At the other end of the scale, the Bearded Collie breed standard requests flat ribs. Between these two extremes fit the oval or egg-shaped chest dimensions of most breeds.
See Rib, **Figure 273a**

CHEST, DEPTH OF; DEEP IN CHEST syn. deep brisket, deep in brisket, deep in ribs. Depth of chest is measured from the withers to the lowest point of the sternum. A dog is spoken of as being 'deep in chest' or 'well-developed in chest depth' if this distance is adequate or correct for its breed. A deep chest usually refers to one that descends at least to the point of the elbow. Conversely, an animal insufficiently deep in chest is said to be 'shallow in chest'.
See **Figure 48**

CHEST MEASUREMENTS
See Chest capacity, Deep in chest, Measurements

CHEST TYPES

Barrel or **barrel-shaped chest**
See Chest capacity, Barrel

Egg-shaped chest syn. oval chest, pear-shaped chest. The normal chest shape for most breeds.

Shallow in chest; shallow chested
See Deep in chest

Well-developed in chest A reference to adequate chest dimensions, i.e., depth, width, and length, for a given breed.
See Chest capacity

Well ribbed up in chest Usually taken in relation to the length of the rib cage, but sometimes employed to denote adequate chest development in general.
See **Figure 273b**

Well sprung chest A reference to rib shape or spring of rib, especially its relation to chest capacity. The opposite to flat, poorly arched or constricted rib development.

CHIN The lower portion of the muzzle, viewed front on, i.e., the area around the junction (symphysis) of the two lower jaw bone halves.
See Jaw, **Figure 11**

Chin whiskers
See Whiskers

CHINA EYE syn. wall eye.
See Eye Colour

CHINESE EYES
See Eye Types, Eyes obliquely placed

CHISELLED; CHISELLING syn. modelling. A request for clean-cut lines and contours, in contrast to bumpy or bulging outlines, especially about the head and foreface. Such construction, particularly if enhanced by fine, close-fitting skin covering, adds to an impression of refinement. References to chiselling abound in breed standards, e.g., 'moderately chiselled' (Smooth Fox Terrier), 'delicate chiselling' (Irish Terrier), 'finely chiselled' (Siberian Husky), etc. **(Figure 56)**.
See **Figure 52**

Fig. 56 Chiselling: Norwegian Puffin Dog

CHOPS A specialist term used in the British Bulldog standard to describe the particularly thick, broad, pendent and very deep flews of this breed **(Figure 57)**.
See Flews

CIRCULAR FEET A requirement of the Sussex Spaniel.
See Feet Types: Cat feet

Fig. 57 Chops: note cushion, turn-up, dewlap, jowls and flews: British Bulldog

CLAW syn. toenail. Occasionally referred to in breed standards, e.g., Dandie Dinmont Terrier.

CLEAN CUT Employed to describe general physical conformation and, in particular, head properties, inferring smooth and trim features, free of lumps, bumps and/or excessive bulges.
See **Figures 52, 214** and **266**

CLEAN IN HEAD
See Head

CLEAR CUT Used in the wording of some breed standards, meaning well-defined, without frills or confusion, unencumbered, unobstructed, etc.

CLEFT PALATE
See Palate, cleft

CLIPPED KEEL
See Keel, clipped

CLODDY Mainly employed in reference to general appearance, e.g., 'cloddy in build' denoting all of thick, heavy set, plain, inelegant, gross or low on leg. Occasionally also used in relation to gait as a synonym for 'clumsy'.

CLOSE-COUPLED syn. short-coupled.
See Coupling

CLOSE-CUPPED FEET
See Feet Types: Cat feet

CLOWN FACE
See Face Types

COARSE; COARSENESS Applied to overall construction, and especially bone, head and/or muscle properties, meaning lack of refinement, heavier, plainer, larger or clumsier physique than desirable. Numerous breed standards list coarseness as a fault, e.g., Australian Silky Terrier, which mentions it along with its opposite 'weediness'. 'Coarse' may also apply to coats, implying a rough or harsh texture.

COARSE SHOULDERS
See Shoulders

COARSE SKULL
See Skull

COAT syn. jacket. The hairy outer covering of the skin. The majority of canine breeds possess two coats: an outer coat and an undercoat. The undercoat is normally short, soft and dense. It assists as a support for the outer coat as well as acting as a weatherproofing blanket. The outer or top coat tends to be longer, harsher and often stand-offish. Breeds carrying both types of coat are termed 'double-coated'. Old English Sheepdogs, German Shepherd Dogs, Lakeland Terriers, etc., serve as examples of double-coated breeds. Single-coated varieties include Italian Greyhounds, Maltese and Pointers.
See **Figures 44** and **279**

Bear-like coat A description applied to the coat of the Eskimo Dog. A double coat consisting of a harsh outer jacket, 7.5 cm to 15 cm (3 in to 6 in) in length, coupled with a soft, dense and woolly undercoat, 2.5 cm to 5 cm (1 in to 2 in) long.

Bristle coat At times used as a synonym of broken- or wire-coated. However, the term more correctly belongs to the coat of the Shar-Pei or Chinese Fighting Dog, which is short, bristly and stiff like that of a pig.

Broken coat syn. wiry coat. Descriptive term for crinkly, harsh and wiry coats, especially those of some Terrier breeds. A broken coat consists of a harsh and often wiry outer jacket plus a dense, softer undercoat. In overall texture it resembles coconut matting. On attaining maximum length, the outer coat tends to soften or 'blow'. At this stage it should be removed, preferably by hand-plucking, to allow for replacement by new, harsh fur **(Figure 58)**.

Fig. 58 Crinkly, broken or wiry coat: Fox Terrier (Wire)

Compact coat
See Compact

Corded coat The unique coat of some breeds, typified by the Hungarian Puli or Komondor, and due to natural intertwining of top and undercoat components. The cords so established may vary in width from quite narrow to broad; they should always be distinct or separate from one another, not matted or joined. Constant attention, i.e., grooming, is required to keep such cords from becoming entangled **(Figure 59)**.

Corded coat (detail)

Fig. 59 Corded coat: Komondor

Crinkly coat Used to describe the slightly waved, harsh coat of the Wire Fox Terrier **(Figure 58)**.
See Broken coat

Curly coat The highly specialised coat of, for example, the Irish Water Spaniel or the Curly-Coated Retriever. A curly coat is a mass of thick, tight curls, resembling astrakhan, which traps air, thus protecting the dog against water and cold.
See **Figure 259**

Double coat syn. two-ply coat.
See Coat

Glossy coat Shiny, lustrous coat, denoting health and well-being.
See **Figures 62** and **266**

Linty coat The unusual, soft, downy type of texture demanded for the Bedlington Terrier's coat. *See* **Figures 174** and **175**

Open coat A sparsely haired coat, the fibres of which are widely separated from one another, usually off-standing and lacking in undercoat. The opposite to tightly packed, flat or compact coats.

Out of coat Applied to long- and/or broken-coated animals that have dropped their outer jackets for one reason or another, e.g., climate, season, ill-health, stress, etc.; also employed to describe normally thick-pelted specimens which for similar reasons have shed their undercoat.

Outer coat
See Coat

Pily coat Applied to describe the peculiar crisp coat texture of the Dandie Dinmont Terrier or Border Collie. Such a jacket consists of a dense and harsh outer coat, coupled with a soft, fur-like and very close inner coat **(Figure 60a)**.

Single coat
See Coat

Fig. 60a Pily coat: Dandie Dinmont Terrier

Fig. 60b Smooth coat: Bull Terrier

Smooth coat Short, close-lying hair, e.g., smooth-coated varieties of Dachshund, Manchester Terrier, Bull Terrier, etc. **(Figure 60b)**.

Stand-off coat Long, heavy and harsh jacket with hair standing out from the body as opposed to lying flat against the skin; usually supported by a shorter, soft, dense undercoat. Typical of Keeshond, Pomeranian, etc. **(Figure 61)**.

Fig. 61 Stand-off coat: Keeshond

Taut coat Actually sleek, tightly stretched skin, devoid of wrinkles, folds and creases, e.g., typical of the German Short-haired Pointer. *See* **Figure 133**

Two-ply coat syn. double coat.

Undercoat
See Coat

Wiry coat
See Broken coat

COBBY Meaning compact, strong, thick-set, chunky and relatively short, both in body length as well as height; taken from 'cob', a short thick-set type of horse. Mentioned as a requirement in some breed standards, e.g., King Charles Spaniel, Maltese, Pug, Japanese Chin, French Bulldog **(Figure 62)**. *See* Compact

Fig. 62 Cobby: Pug. Also described as compact or multum in parvo

COCCYGEAL VERTEBRAE
See Spinal column

COCKED-UP TAIL
See Tail Types

COFFIN HEAD
See Head Types

COLLAR Coat marking around the neck, usually white. Typified by breeds such as the Collie, Basenji, Old English Sheepdog, etc. For further clarification, collars are often described as wide or narrow, complete or incomplete, broken, etc. **(Figure 63)**.

Fig. 63 Collar: Basenji

Collar, royal The well-developed, symmetrical and evenly placed full white collar of some breeds, e.g., Old English Sheepdog **(Figure 64)**. See **Figure 44**

COLLARETTE The relatively slight ruff formation round the neck of the Belgian Malinois.

COLOUR, BREAKING syn. clearing colour; colour in the process of breaking or clearing. The changing of coat colour during the transition phase of puppyhood into adulthood, e.g., black into blue in the Kerry Blue Terrier and Australian Silky Terrier.

COLOUR, BROKEN A dog whose solid coat colour is broken up in continuity by patches of another colour, frequently white.

COLOUR, CLEARING
See Colour, breaking

COMMISURES The lip corners, i.e., the meeting of the lower and upper lip edges at the sides of the muzzle.
See **Figures 201 and 362**

Fig. 64 Royal collar: Old English Sheepdog

COMMUNAL PAD syn. metacarpal pad.
See Feet Anatomy

COMPACT Although the words 'compact' and 'cobby' are frequently used in synonymous fashion, they do, in fact, describe different physical aspects. 'Compact' refers to the union of various body parts, i.e., firmly joined. 'Cobby', on the other hand, relates to overall body shape, i.e., height to body length proportions (see **Figure 62**). For example, the Japanese Chin standard states that 'body should be squarely and compactly built plus be cobby in shape', whilst the Siberian Husky standard demands an appearance from 'moderately compact (but never cobby) to moderately rangy' **(Figure 65)**.
'Compact' is also used to describe a short to medium length coat, very close-lying, with a dense undercoat and giving a smooth outline.

COMPACT FEET
See Feet Types

CONDITION An animal's state of fitness or health as reflected by external appearance and behaviour. For example, muscular development, state/gloss of coat, expression, etc., are all outward signs or pointers of well-being or good condition.

CONFORMATION Overall appearance and structure determined by the physical develop-

Fig. 65 Compact: Siberian Husky

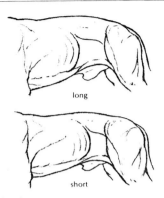

Fig. 66 Coupling

ment of an animal's individual parts as well as the combined relationship and outlines of such.

CONGENITAL A feature, usually a defect, which is present at birth, e.g., cleft palate, in contrast to an inherited one which develops later, e.g., progressive retinal atrophy.

CONJUNCTIVA The mucous membrane lining of both upper or lower eyelids. Of pinkish coloration, the conjunctivae are not visible under normal circumstances in most breeds. Exceptions include the Bloodhound, Saint Bernard, etc., in which the breed standards request a certain degree of lower lid looseness. Animals with loose or everted lower eyelids are referred to as 'showing haw' or being 'haw-eyed'. In veterinary terms such a condition is known as ectropion.
See Haw, **Figures 116, 164** and **165**

CORDED COAT
See Coat, corded

CORKSCREW TAIL
See Tail Types

CORKY Infrequently used expression to denote lively, spunky temperament.

COUPLING; COUPLINGS The junction of the chest to the hindquarters. At the top, the region of the coupling consists of the lumbar section of the vertebral column, together with the associated loin muscles. To the sides, the loins join into the abdominal wall and flank regions; at its lower edge the coupling blends with the abdominal floor. The coupling is in fact the whole muscular band joining the chest and hindquarters, not just the loin area.
   A dog is termed 'short-coupled' or 'close-coupled' when the distance between the last rib and the commencement of the hindquarters section is relatively short and therefore strong. Conversely, it is 'long-coupled', 'long in coupling' or 'loosely coupled' if such a distance is long **(Figure 66)**. While reasonable length of coupling is required for turning ability, long loins and/or coupling generally tend to be regarded as a structural weakness.

COUPLINGS, OPEN Unusual terminology, employed in the Flat-Coated Retriever breed standard, for long loins and flanks insufficiently well-muscled.

COVERING GROUND An expression with two basic meanings. When the dog is standing, it refers to the distance between front and hind legs, i.e., a synonym of standing over a lot of ground. When moving, it means easy, economical action with maximum stride, length or reach.

COW HOCKS, COW HOCKED
See Hocks, cow

COW HOCKED GAIT or **ACTION**
See Gait, Hocks

COWLICK A tuft, whirl or twist of hair, sticking up and facing in a direction different to that of the surrounding coat, i.e., as if licked up by a cow's tongue.

CRABBING
See Gait

CRANK TAIL or **STERN**
See Tail Types

CREASELESS Schnauzer breed standard terminology meaning freedom from wrinkles and/or skin folds about the head.

CREST Usually a reference to the upper margin of the neck. Commencing at the head/neck junction (nape) and ending at the neck/withers blend-in, such an arch tends to be most marked in adult male animals. 'Crest' is also used to describe the long, sparse hair tufts about the head and neck of the Chinese Crested Dog **(Figure 67)**.
See **Figure 11**

Fig. 67 Crest: Chinese Crested Dog

CRESTED NECK
See Neck Types

CRINKLY COAT
See Coat

CROOK A term employed primarily to describe the forequarters assembly of some short-legged breeds with inwards inclining pasterns, e.g., Basset Hound, Dachshund. When viewed front on, the crook of such animals actually cradles the chest **(Figure 68)**. 'Crook' is also used to describe the terminal swirl in the tail of the Briard (A.K.C. breed standard) **(Figure 322)**.
See **Figure 322**

Fig. 68 Crook: achondroplastic limbs

CROOK TAIL
See Crook, Tail Types

CROOKED FRONT
See Front Types

CROOKED MOUTH
See Mouth

CROP The surgical removal of a portion of the ear cartilage. Such an operation is usually performed at ten to sixteen weeks of age in order to make normally drop or pendent ears stand erect. Great Danes, Dobermanns and Schnauzers are good examples of 'cropped' breeds. Used as a noun, 'crop' refers to the effect obtained by surgical removal of the ear cartilage. Because it is regarded as unnecessarily cruel, since today this operation is carried out only for aesthetic purposes, ear cropping has been declared illegal in Australia as well as England and numerous other European countries. However, it is still a permitted surgical procedure in most parts of the U.S.A.

The origin of ear cropping dates back to problems encountered by owners of working dogs in Europe in early times. Ear cropping in those days was carried out not for cosmetic reasons, but rather to prevent or at least to minimise injuries caused by fighting natural enemies preying upon flocks and herds and/or harsh working conditions; also in some cases to improve hearing in drop-eared working breeds. Before dog fighting became outlawed as a national 'sport', ears were also cropped to prevent serious injury during combat.
See **Figure 87**

CROPPED EARS
See Ear Types

CROSS BRED syn. cross breed.
See Mongrel

CROUCH An unnatural gathering-up of the hindquarters due to excessive hind limbs angulation, or in some cases to insecure temperament. The result is a markedly sloping and arched backline, in which the rump/croup section, when viewed in profile, appears appreciably lower than the forequarters **(Figure 69)**.
See Droop

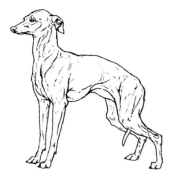
Fig. 69 Crouch: Italian Greyhound

CROUP The muscular area just above and around the set-on of the tail. It merges into the rump in front and technically overlies the lower half of the pelvic region, i.e., from the hip joints to the buttocks. Many variations of croup (often alluded to as rump) formation are described in the breed standards, e.g., flat, steep, long, short, rounded, sunken, slightly hollow, etc. **(Figure 70)**.

Croup, sunken One that is concave in outline due to inadequate muscle covering. An undesirable feature in any breed.
See Rump

gently rounded continuation of the backline: correct tail set and no line of demarcation

goose rump: low set tail

high-set tail (steer tail) flat croup

falling away, steep croup

Fig. 70 Croups and tail sets

CROWN syn. dome, topskull. A noun with three basic meanings: (a) the roof of the brain case formed by the fusion of frontal, parietal and occipital bones, e.g., 'pronounced roundness of crown (dome)' (American Cocker Spaniel) **(Figure 294)** (b) the geometrical pattern at the start of the Rhodesian Ridgeback's ridge **(Figure 71)** (c) that part of a tooth above the gum line **(Figure 74)**.
See Dentition, Skull, domed

Fig. 71 Ridge and crown: Rhodesian Ridgeback

CRUPPER Borrowed from horse terminology, a term used to describe the croup, especially that part near the tail insertion, e.g., 'slanting crupper' mentioned as a fault in the Schnauzer breed standard.

CRYPTORCHID; CRYPTORCHIDISM A male dog in which one or both testicles has/have not descended properly into the scrotum. Under normal circumstances the testicles of male puppies, embryologically having developed high up inside the abdomen, are located either in or near the scrotum at birth, or reach that area within the first three weeks of age. Animals with both testicles normally descended are referred to as being 'entire'. Those in which one testicle remains undescended are spoken of as being unilateral cryptorchids (or at times incorrectly as monorchids). Dogs with both testicles retained inside the body cavity are termed bilateral cryptorchids. The condition of testicular retention is known as cryptorchidism. It is thought to have an hereditary basis.

CUFFS The short-haired pastern regions, front and/or rear, on the so-called 'bare-pasterned' Afghan Hound variety.
See Pastern, **Figure 257a**

CULOTTE syn. breeches, trousering. The specific name given to the longish hair, trousering or breeching at the rear upper thigh region of the Schipperke.
See **Figure 46a**

CURLY COAT
See Coat Types

CURTAIN
See Veil, **Figure 359**

CUSHION; CUSHIONING syn. padding. Refers to exceptional thickness of upper lips or flews. A highly desirable feature of some breeds, e.g., Boxer, British Bulldog, Pekingese **(Figure 72, see Figures 57, 255 and 275)**. The term cushion is also applied to the canine foot, thickly developed foot pads being referred to as 'well-cushioned'.
See Feet Anatomy and **Figure 125**

CUT-UP
See Tuck-up

Fig. 72 Cushion: Boxer

D

Fig. 73 Dapple: Dachshund

DAPPLE A spotted, mottled or variegated coat colour pattern involving darker, irregular markings on a lighter ground. Sometimes used synonymously with merle **(Figure 73)**.

DEAD EARS
See Ear Types

DEADGRASS A coat colour varying in shade from tan to dull straw, referred to in the Chesapeake Bay Retriever breed standard (A.K.C.).

DEEP IN CHEST
See Chest, deep in

DEEP IN BRISKET
See Brisket: Deep brisket

DEEP IN RIBS
See Ribs

DEEP THROUGH THE HEART An unusual expression, meaning a good depth of chest, e.g., Golden Retriever breed standard.

DENTITION A noun (derived from the Latin *dens, dentis*: tooth) referring to the kind and number of teeth characteristic of a species, as well as to their arrangement in the jaws. The teeth of the dog are highly specialised structures, consisting of a crown (the exposed part above the gum), a neck (at the gum line), and a root (embedded in the jaw bone). They are constructed of enamel (the pearly-white outer covering of the crown), dentine (the tooth bulk beneath the enamel coating), cementum (a thin bone-like substance spread over the roots) and pulp (the soft tissue composed of sensory nerves, blood vessels, etc.) **(Figure 74)**.

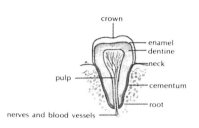

Fig. 74 Anatomy of a tooth

Dogs, like humans, grow two sets of teeth during their lifetime. The first, in puppyhood, is deciduous or temporary. Occasionally referred to as baby or milk teeth, these appear from about three weeks of age and consist of twenty-eight teeth, i.e., twelve incisors, four canines and twelve premolars. From about two to three months of age to approximately six to seven months, the milk teeth are gradually replaced by a full set of forty-two permanent teeth. Because the eruption times of permanent teeth are more or less constant, they can be used in age estimation.

In classification, the teeth of dogs are divided into four groups: incisors, canines, premolars and molars **(Figures 75 and 76)**. The incisors are the smallish teeth in front, and number twelve, i.e., six in each of the upper and lower jaws. They are relatively long, slender in shape, and slightly arched in a forward direction. All twelve incisors are present in the deciduous set and are eventually replaced by their permanent counterparts. The anatomical relationship between the upper and lower incisors at their point of contact forms the so-called 'bite', e.g., scissors, pincer, etc.

The canines (syn. fangs, holders, eye teeth, tusks) are four in number. Two are located in each of the upper and lower jaws, next to the respective corner incisors. The areas between the two upper canines, as well as that between the two lower canines, occupied by their respective rows of incisor teeth, are referred to as the dental arches. The canine teeth are by far the longest and strongest in the dog's mouth. Their roots are almost twice as long as the crowns. In shape they tend to be slightly curved, compressed from side to side and bluntly pointed at the tips. The tem-

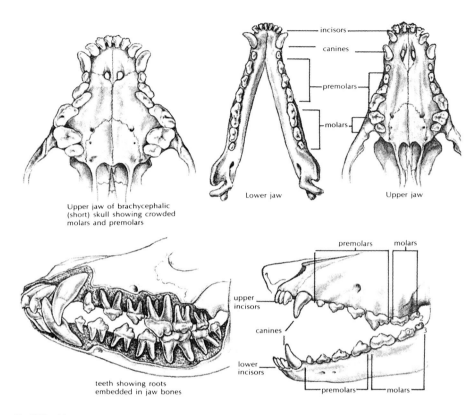

Upper jaw of brachycephalic (short) skull showing crowded molars and premolars

Lower jaw

Upper jaw

incisors

canines

premolars

molars

premolars molars

upper incisors

canines

lower incisors

premolars molars

teeth showing roots embedded in jaw bones

Fig. 75 Dentition

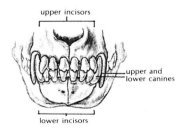

upper incisors

upper and lower canines

lower incisors

Fig. 76 Dentition

porary canine teeth have usually erupted by four weeks of age. They are replaced by permanent ones at about five to six months.

The premolars are situated at the sides of the jaws, behind the canine teeth and in front of the molars. Both upper and lower jaws contain a complement of eight premolars. The first premolar is the smallest, with size increasing towards the last or fourth premolar. The carnassial or sectorial tooth is the name given to the fourth premolar in the upper jaw and the first molar in the lower jaw.

See **Figure 51**

The molars are the rearmost teeth of both jaws. They number six for the lower jaw and four for the upper jaw. Unlike the other teeth groupings, there are no molars in the deciduous dentition.

Although the full dentition of forty-two teeth is considered most desirable in show dogs (a number of breed standards, in fact, do mention it, e.g., the Poodle) it is not unusual for dogs to have missing teeth. Those most commonly absent are the premolars. This is really not surprising when it is realised, from skulls discovered at ancient excavation sites, that the first three premolars in each jaw were absent in most prehistoric specimens. This phenomenon is still apparent in hairless breeds such as the Chinese Crested Dog and the Mexican Hairless Dog, in which all the premolars are usually absent.
See Jaws, Bite

DEPTH OF CHEST
See Chest, depth of

DEWCLAWS
Front dewclaws The rather under-developed, degenerate first metacarpal bone and associated phalanges, located on the inner surface of the pastern region.
See Feet Anatomy, **Figure 125,** Forequarters

Rear dewclaws syn. wolf's claw, spur. When present, the rudimentary first metatarsal bone and associated phalanges are located on the innermost surface of the rear pastern. In most breeds the rear dewclaw is either absent at birth, or, when present, is removed soon afterwards. It is, however, an essential requirement of some breeds, either in single and occasionally even in double form. In the Briard and Pyrenean Mountain Dog, for example, the presence of double rear dewclaws, apart from offering assistance whilst working in rough terrain, supposedly denotes superior breeding.
The Norwegian Lundehund or Puffin Dog has double dewclaws on all four legs. It is, in fact, the only breed in the world with five fully-developed toes on each foot, which assists it in climbing rocky cliffs inaccessible to man, to seek out Puffin birds.
See Feet Anatomy, **Figure 125**

DEWLAP The loose, pendulous skin, usually arranged in folds, on the chin, throat and neck regions of some breeds, e.g., Bloodhound, Basset Hound **(Figure 77).**
See **Figures 57, 197** and **237**

Fig. 77 Dewlap: Bloodhound

DIAMOND syn. thumb mark. The characteristically shaped black mark on the forehead of the fawn-coloured Pug variety **(Figure 78).**

Fig. 78 Diamond: Pug

DIAPHRAGM
See Body

DIGIT syn. toe.
See Feet Anatomy

DIP or **DIPPED** or **DIPPY BACK** syn. hollow back.
See Back Types

DISCS, INTERVERTEBRAL
See Intervertebral Discs

DISH FACE or FACED
See Face

DISHING
See Gait

DISTEMPER TEETH Damaged, discoloured teeth due to incomplete or pitted enamel covering. Despite their rather specific name, distemper teeth may be caused by any serious setback, e.g., incorrect nutrition, parasitism or disease (due to prolonged rise in temperature) during their developmental and eruption phases.
See Dentition

DOCK To cut or adjust tail length, normally at between four to five days of age. Typically docked breeds include Dobermanns, Fox Terriers, Boxers, etc. Used as a noun, 'dock' refers to the length of a surgically adjusted tail, e.g., a tail of correct dock.
See **Figure 318**

DOLICHOCEPHALIC
See Skull Types

DOME
See Crown

DOMED SKULL
See Skull Types

DOMINO Reverse facial mask pattern on the head of some breeds, e.g., Afghan Hound **(Figure 79).**
See Widow's Peak and Cap, **Figure 50**

Fig. 79 Domino: Saluki

DORSAL Anatomical terminology for 'on or near the back'. The opposite to ventral.

DOUBLE-JOINTEDNESS An anatomical abnormality mentioned in numerous breed standards (especially in relation to the hock joint) and referring to joints capable of movement outside normal parameters. A mild form of this condition is not infrequently described as 'slipped' hocks.

DOWN FACE or **FACED**
See Face

DOWN IN PASTERN
See Pastern

DRAPES
See Hair, Fall of

DRIVE; DRIVING POWER Used to describe hindquarter propulsion. Dogs with powerful rear action are sometimes referred to as having 'plenty of drive', e.g., Cocker Spaniel breed standard.

DROOP Slope (usually excessive) of the croup region, e.g., 'hindquarters drooping' (Scottish Deerhound breed standard) **(Figure 80)**.

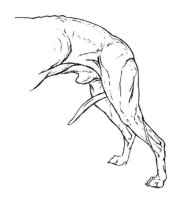

Fig. 80 Droop: hindquarters

DROP or **DROPPED EARS**
See Ear Types

DRY An adjective most frequently employed to describe relative freedom from wrinkles and folds, i.e., taut skin on head, neck or body. More recently, 'dry', as a direct translation from the German *trocken*, has found use amongst German Shepherd fanciers for hard, lean physical condition.

DRY NECK
See Neck Types

DUDLEY In the British Bulldog breed standard, 'dudley' refers to unpigmented nose colour, also to body colouring as a whole. It is undesirable in either form.
See Nose Types: Dudley nose

E

EAR ANATOMY The canine ear consists of three parts: the external ear or auricle, the middle ear and the inner ear. To dog judges, breeders and fanciers, the ear lobe, pinna or leather is of prime importance. Its size, shape, thickness, attachment, carriage, mobility, etc., all tend to be characteristic of individual breeds, and hence exert great influence upon 'expression'.

Each lobe consists of auricular cartilage, covered on both sides by skin **(Figure 81)**. The outer covering is furry; the inner one usually smooth. Ear carriage and/or mobility is influenced by a number of factors, not the least of which are the various individual muscle groups attaching the base of the ear to the sides of the skull **(Figure 82)**. The point of junction of ear lobe to head is referred to as the 'set-on'. From there, the shape of the cartilage changes to form the funnel-shaped external ear canal. At first this runs vertically downwards for some distance, then turns at a right angle to continue in the direction of the eardrum **(Figure 83)**. The basic function of the ear lobe, especially when carried erect, is to receive air vibrations, i.e., sound waves, much as a radio antenna does. It ducts these via the external ear canal to the eardrum, middle ear, and finally to the inner ear for reception. Ear lobe size, shape and carriage vary enormously from breed to breed.
See Ear Types

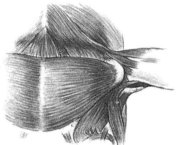

Muscles between the ears

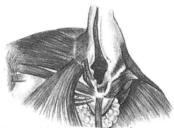

Muscles around the base of the ear
(ear somewhat folded up)

Fig. 82 Muscles surrounding the ear

EAR, BREAK OF The line of crease or fold in a semi-drop ear, e.g., Fox Terrier **(Figures 84 and 86)**.

EAR CARRIAGE The combined visual effects of ear placement and position on the skull, coupled with usage. Many adjectives are used to describe canine ear carriage, e.g., lazy, drop, alert, dead or upright.
See Ear Types

EAR FEATHER or **FRINGES**
See Feather, Fringe

EAR LEATHER
See Leather, Ear Anatomy

EAR LOBE syn. leather, pinna.
See Ear Anatomy

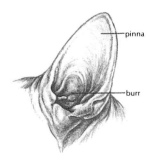

pinna

burr

Fig. 81 Ear anatomy

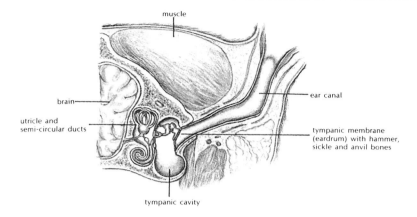

Fig. 83 Anatomy of ear canal and inner ear

Fig. 84 Button ears: Lakeland Terrier

EAR TYPES Many in number, the ear shapes of dogs may generally be grouped under three headings: (a) Erect or pricked, e.g., German Shepherd Dog, West Highland White Terrier, (b) Drop, pendent or pendulous, e.g., Spaniel breeds, Dachshund, Poodle, (c) Semi-drop or semi-prick, e.g., Collie, Fox Terrier.

Great variations occur within the framework of these three classifications, between breeds as well as individuals due to set-on, position, shape, size, thickness and/or carriage of the ear lobes. The descriptive nomenclature employed in the breed standards adds further confusion. The most common types of ear found in the canine species are listed below.

Bat ears
See Ear Types: Tulip ear

Bear ears A very round-tipped ear, mentioned as a fault in the A.K.C.'s Samoyed breed standard.

Blunt-tipped ears syn. round-tipped ears. Ear lobe shape as typified by the French Bulldog, Chow,

Chow, Cardigan Welsh Corgi, etc., in contrast to sharp- or pointed-tipped ears, e.g., Yorkshire Terrier.
See **Figures 99a, 100** and **103**

Broken or **broken-down ears** Deformed, misshapen ears caused by injury or abnormal construction of the ear cartilage; mentioned in many breed standards as a fault, e.g., Chihuahua, or as a disqualification (A.K.C.'s version of the Akita standard).

Button ears A semi-erect type in which the lower lobe portion stands upright with the top part dropped or folded forward in the direction of the eye, thereby at least partially obscuring the external ear canal's orifice, e.g., Fox Terrier, Irish Terrier **(Figure 84)**.

Candle flame ears A description specific to the individualistic flame-shaped ears of the English Toy Terrier **(Figure 85)**.

Fig. 85 Candle flame ears: English Toy Terrier

Fig. 86 Break of ear, cocked ears, semi-droop or semi-prick ears: Shetland Sheepdog

Cocked ears syn. semi-drop, semi-prick. Erect ears in which the tip only is bent forwards. Also known as 'tipped ears' **(Figure 86)**.

Crop or cropped ears Natural drop ears made to stand erect by the surgical removal of a portion of the ear lobe. Examples of breeds frequently cropped include Dobermann, Great Dane, Schnauzer. While the operation of ear cropping was permitted at the time of writing in most parts of the U.S.A., South America and some European countries, it is illegal in the United Kingdom, Australia and Scandinavia. More and more countries may ban ear-cropping in the future **(Figure 87)**.

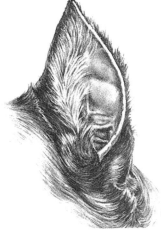

Fig. 87 Cropped ear: Dobermann

Dead ears Relatively immobile, sluggish ears, poorly responsive to external stimuli. 'A "dead" ear, hound-like in appearance', for example, is listed as a fault in the Kerry Blue Terrier standard as well as in the Irish Terrier's A.K.C. breed standard.

Drop or dropped ears syn. folded ears, full drop ears, hanging ears, pendent ears, pendulous ears. The opposite to erect ears, i.e., those that hang down from their area of junction to the head, as in Setter and Spaniel breeds and Retrievers. In normally erect-eared dogs, the term 'drop ear' refers to one that shows any deviation from the fully upright position, e.g., Chow Chow breed standard (A.K.C.) which lists drop ears as a fault, then goes on to explain that 'a drop ear is one that is stiffly carried or stiffly erect, but which breaks over at any point from its base to its tip' **(Figure 88)**.

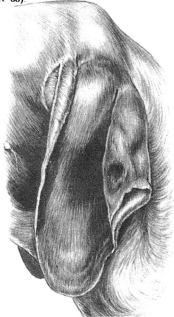

Fig. 88 Hound ear: drop, pendulous, folded and set on low: Basset Hound

Erect ears syn. prick or pricked ears, upright ears. Stiff upstanding ears, as in the German Shepherd Dog, Pomeranian, Belgian Malinois, Siberian Husky, etc. They may be blunt- or pointed-tipped **(Figures 85 and 89)**.

Filbert-shaped ears The individualistic shape demanded for the ear lobes of the Bedlington Terrier. The term comes from the shape of the hazel nut or filbert **(Figure 90)**.

Fleshy ears Those constructed of thicker cartilage than desirable, and/or covered with too-coarse skin. Mentioned as a fault in the German Shorthaired Pointer breed standard.

Fig. 89 Erect or pricked ears: German Shepherd Dog

Fig. 91 Flying ears: Whippet

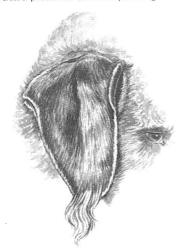

Fig. 90 Filbert-shaped ears: Bedlington Terrier

Fig. 92 Rolled, folded and curled-in ears low set: Bloodhound

Flop ears Normally erect ears which, for one reason or another, have flopped, dropped or failed to stand erect.

Fly or **Flying ears** Terminology applied to (a) normally drop ears, one or both of which, instead of hanging correctly close to the cheek as required by the breed standard, tend to stick out or 'fly away' from the sides of the face (b) incorrect and incomplete erection of ears in normally prick-eared breeds (c) the correct position assumed by the ears of gazehounds when brought to attention.

Regarding incorrect carriage, fly or flying ears may be a permanent affliction, e.g., due to excessively thick ear lobe cartilage or incorrect set-on, or be of a transient nature only, e.g., caused by teething, illness or aberrant temperament, etc. **(Figure 91)**.

Folded ears Pendent or drop ears in which the lobes hang in longitudinal folds rather than lying

perfectly flat, e.g., Bloodhound, Field Spaniel **(Figure 92)**.

Full drop ears
See Ear Types: Drop ears

Hanging ears
See Ear Types: Drop ears

Heart-shaped ears The self-explanatory desirable shape of ear cartilage referred to in the breed standards of the Pekingese, Tibetan Mastiff, Portuguese Water Dog, etc. **(Figure 93)**.

High set ears Ears, the origin of which is near the top of the skull, or at least above eye level, e.g., British Bulldog **(Figure 97b)**, in contrast to the opposite arrangement, e.g., Bloodhound **(Figure 92)**.

Hooded ears Smallish ears in which both lobe edges curve forwards markedly, e.g., Basenji, Chow Chow **(Figure 94)**.

Fig. 93 Heart-shaped ears: Pekingese

Fig. 94 Hooded ears: Basenji

Fig. 95 Inward constricted ears

Fig. 96 Propeller ears

Hound or **hound-like ears** Used in some breed standards, particularly those of the Terrier group, to describe a full drop ear, which in a given breed is considered faulty, e.g., 'a pendulous ear, hanging dead by the side of the head like a hound's, is a fault' (Airedale Terrier) **(Figure 88)**.

Inward constricted ears Ear lobes that are normally required to be carried vertically upright, but which, due to weak attachment of the inner edges to the skull, angle in towards the centre line, sometimes even touching each other. This is often of a temporary nature only and common during the process of ear erection in pups. One or both ears may be affected **(Figure 95)**.

Lobular or **lobe-shaped ears** The ear lobe shape requested for the English Springer Spaniel, Irish Water Spaniel, and Cocker Spaniel.
See **Figure 212**

Low set ears
See Ear Types: High set ears

Pendent or **pendulous ears**
See Ear Types: Drop ears

Prick or **pricked ears**
See Ear Types: Erect ears

Propeller ears Ears which, instead of being carried correctly, stick out sideways in more or less horizontal, propeller-like fashion. Similar to fly ears **(Figure 96)**.

Rolled ears syn. ears curled inwards. Long, pendent, folded, hound type ears which are rolled or curled inwards along the lower edge and tip, e.g., Field Spaniel, Bloodhound **(Figure 92)**.

Rose ears Smallish drop ears that fold over and back so as to expose the burr; typical of Pug, Whippet and Bulldog **(Figures 97a and 97b)**.

Round-tipped ears
See Ear Types: Blunt-tipped ears

Semi-drop or **semi-prick ears** syn. cocked ears, tipped ears. Basically erect ears, with just the tips drooping forwards, as exemplified by the Collie and Shetland Sheepdog **(Figure 86)**.

Sharp-tipped ears syn. pointed-tipped ears.
See Ear Types: Blunt-tipped ears, **Figure 85**

Triangular ears
See Ear Types: V-shaped ears

Trowel-shaped ears An unusual shape of lobe requested in the Stabyhoun **(Figure 98)**.

Tulip ears Not infrequently confused with bat ears, mainly because of differences in terminology interpretation between European and English authorities. Most European sources define tulip ears as stiffly upright with edges curved slightly forwards so as closely to resemble a tulip petal in shape, e.g., French Bulldog **(Figure 99a)**. English writers, on the other hand, define tulip ears as ears normally rose or semi-drop, but which for some reason are more or less erect with edges curved markedly forwards and inwards. Tulip ears fitting this description, for example, are listed as faults in the British Bulldog and Wire-haired Fox Terrier breed standards **(Figure 99b)**.

Fig. 97a Rose ear: Whippet

Fig 97b High-set rose ears: British Bulldog

Fig. 98 Trowel-shaped ears: Stabyhoun

Fig. 99a Tulip ears: high and close set: French Bulldog

Fig. 99b Tulip ears: British Bulldog

Bat ears, according to the European definition, resemble tulip ears closely in that they are fully erect, wide and facing forwards, rounded at the tips, set relatively wide on the skull, broad at the base and carried out from the head at a slight angle, e.g., Cardigan Welsh Corgi, in contrast to the more upright carriage of the French Bulldog **(Figure 100)**.

Fig. 100 Bat ears: blunt and rounded tips, wide set: Welsh Corgi (Cardigan)

Upright ears
See Ear Types: Erect ears

V-shaped ears Refers to triangular-shaped ears, usually, but not always, carried in dropped fashion. The distance from base to tip is relatively long. Similar ears, but shorter in length and usually carried upright, are referred to as triangular. Breed examples include (a) V-shaped: Bullmastiff, Hungarian Puli, Hungarian Vizsla (b) Triangular: Siberian Husky, Samoyed, Belgian Tervueren ('equilateral triangle'), Norwegian Buhund, Pyrenean Mountain Dog, Schipperke, Alaskan Malamute ('upper halves are triangular in shape') **(Figures 101a and 101b)**.

Fig. 101a V-shaped triangular ear: Spitz type

Fig. 101b V-shaped ear showing burr

EARS, SET-ON The junction of ear lobe base to skull. Description of ear set-on is usually related to eye level and/or skull width. Ears joining the skull above eye level are generally referred to as 'set on high', e.g., Great Dane, Siberian Husky. (*See* **Figures 50** and **89**) Conversely, those joining below eye level are termed 'set on low', e.g., Basset Hound and King Charles Spaniel **(Figure 104a;** *see* **Figures 88** and **178)**. Ears wide apart at the base, whether due to actual skull width or type of set, are described as 'set on wide' **(Figure 104b)**.
See Ear Anatomy

Fig. 104a Ears set on low: King Charles Spaniel

Fig. 102 Vine-leaf ear: Welsh Springer Spaniel

Fig. 103 Blunt or round-tipped ear: Chow Chow

Vine-leaf ears The specific lobe shape referred to in the Welsh Springer Spaniel breed standard **(Figure 102)**.

EARS CLOSELY SET The opposite to 'ears set on wide' **(Figures 99a** and **100)**.
See Ears, Set-on

EARS SENSITIVE IN USE Unusual terminology employed in the Australian Terrier breed standard as a pointer to that breed's acute sense of hearing, shown by rapid response of ear carriage and movement to stimulation.

Fig. 104b Ears set on wide: German Shepherd Dog

EARS SET ON LOW or **HIGH** or **WIDE**
See Ears, Set-on

EAST-WEST FEET
See Feet Types

EAST-WEST FRONT
See Front Types

EAST-WEST MOVERS
See Action

ECTROPION The scientific term for exceedingly loose lower eyelids or 'haw-eyedness'.
See Haw

ELBOW; ELBOW JOINT The joint in the forelimb created by the articulation of the humerus (arm) above and the tibia/fibula (forearm) below.
See Forequarters, **Figures 18** and **105**

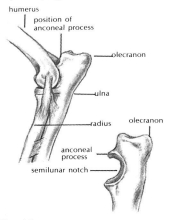

Fig. 105 Elbow joint

ELBOWS, LOOSE IN
See Elbows, Out at

ELBOWS, OUT AT or **OUT IN** Under normal circumstances, a dog's elbows, when standing naturally, are in relatively close proximity to the adjoining chest wall, i.e., well held in, but not so tightly as to restrict movement. An animal in which one or both elbows drift some distance away from the chest wall is referred to as being 'out in elbow or elbows', 'out at elbow or elbows' or 'loose in elbow or elbows'. Such an affliction, apart from being unsightly, often leads to an unsound, energy wasting and excessively tiring gait (see **Figure 144**).

The opposite phenomenon, i.e., elbows placed too firmly up against the chest wall, and often associated with a front in which the distance between the wrists and/or feet is greater than that between the elbows, may be alluded to as 'tied-in elbows'. Such anatomical construction is equally undesirable.

ELBOW, POINT OF
See Forequarters

ELBOWS, TIED IN
See Elbows, Out in

ELBOWS, WELL HELD IN
See Elbows, Out at

ENDURANCE A highly desirable quality, synonymous with stamina, exercise tolerance, performance, etc., required in many breeds, especially working dogs. Endurance fundamentally relates to three areas (a) physical construction, particularly lung and heart room, so necessary for maximum oxygen intake, (b) general anatomical soundness and muscular development, (c) physical fitness.

ENTIRE A reference to testicular normality. A dog with two normal testes, fully descended into the scrotum, is said to be entire, or is an entire dog.
See Cryptorchid

ENTROPION An anatomical abnormality due to spasm and contraction of the muscles controlling the eye rims. This, in consequence, causes the affected eyelids to turn and roll in towards the eyeball. The resultant contact of eyelash to eyeball produces a state of semi-permanent irritation, indicated by squinting, excessive tear flow, etc. Both upper and/or lower eyelids may be affected, the lower more frequently. Furthermore, the problem may be unilateral or bilateral, i.e., it may occur on one or both sides **(Figure 106)**.

The opposite to ectropion, entropion may be congenital (unusual) or develop later in life. Most cases of entropion seen in dogs appear to be of genetic origin, e.g., Chow Chow. Medical treatment, apart from alleviating pain, is of little value. Surgical correction affords the only permanent cure.

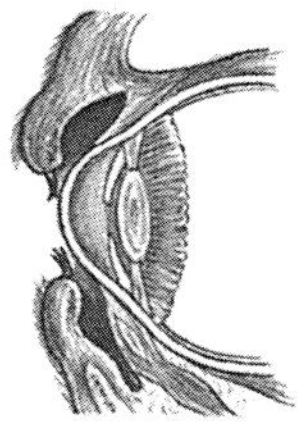

Fig. 106 Entropion

ERECT EARS
See Ear Types

EWE NECK
See Neck Types

EXPRESSION The look, facial expression or countenance typical of some breeds and/or individuals, obtained by the interaction of numerous physical qualities, e.g., ears, eyes, coat, etc., as well as temperament. The breed standards abound with references to expression, e.g., Eastern or Oriental expression (Afghan Hound), grave (Field Spaniel, A.K.C.), ape-like (Tibetan Spaniel), lordly (Chow Chow), intelligent (Samoyed, A.K.C.). The majority are self-explanatory.

Eastern or **Oriental expression** Used in the Afghan Hound standard to describe the illusion created by the combined effects of head structure, eye shape and placement, colour and masking, plus, on occasions, the presence of a beard, which result in this breed's unique countenance **(Figure 107)**.

Fig. 107 Oriental or Eastern expression: Afghan Hound

Frowning expression
See Brows

Gruff expression A specific description of facial characteristics in the Bouvier des Flandres (A.K.C. breed standard), suggesting a tough, hard-bitten appearance, enhanced by bushy eyebrows, moustache and beard.

Monkey-like expression syn. ape-like expression. The distinctive apish facial qualities of some breeds, typified by the Affenpinscher, Griffon Bruxellois and Tibetan Spaniel **(Figure 108)**.

Fig. 108 Apish or monkey-like expression: Affenpinscher

Saucy expression Used to describe the Chihuahua's uniquely piquant or pert facial properties, due basically to a combination of skull and foreface shapes, enhanced by the position, size, etc., of both ears and eyes.
See **Figure 167**

Sombre expression A faulty attribute mentioned in the Boxer breed standard, due in part to masking which, instead of being restricted to the face (as is desirable), spreads onto the skull area, and/or masking which, rather than being clearly delineated, blends indistinctly with the surrounding head colour. Excessive development of head and face wrinkles helps to accentuate such sombre expression.

EXTENSION
See Flexion

EYE ANATOMY The canine eye, in many respects, is similar to that of man. The accompanying diagram **(Figure 109)** depicts its anatomy. In function it resembles a camera. Rays of light impinge upon and penetrate the cornea in front, are brought into focus by the lens located immediately behind the iris diaphragm, and are finally projected onto the light-sensitive retina at the back of the orb or eyeball. The image formed in that area is in turn transported to the brain via the optic nerves for visual impact and recognition. The eyes of dogs exhibit great variation in size and shape as well as in position, according to breed. In the Pekingese or Pug, for example, they seem comparatively large; in the Collie, on the other hand, they are on the small side. The apparent size of eye is governed by a number of factors. Of these, depth of orbit in the skull, actual eyeball dimensions and eyelid development are the most important. The same influences affect eye shape. The eyeball as such is always rounded or nearly so; the variations demanded by some breed standards, e.g., oval (Norfolk Terrier), almond-shaped (Dobermann), triangular (Bedlington Terrier), round (Griffon Bruxellois), etc., are brought about by the factors already mentioned. The iris is of particular importance to breeders, judges, etc., because of its relation to eye colour.
See Eye Colour

Three eyelids help to protect the eyeball from injury; they are identified as upper, lower and third eyelid (or nictitating membrane). The upper and lower eyelids converge and join at their inner and outer corners (medial and lateral angles or canthi). When the lids are open, the space between them is known as the palpebral fissure or aperture. The usually well-developed third eyelid is located at the inner angle (medial canthus) of the palpebral fissure.
See **Figure 349**, Third eyelid

EYEBROWS syn. brows. The skin and hair above the eyes, covering the projecting superciliary ridges or supraorbital processes of the skull's frontal bones **(Figure 110)**. The eyebrows of dogs vary greatly, both in extent or development and prominence as well as in the amount of hair car-

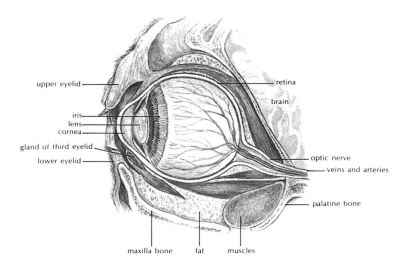

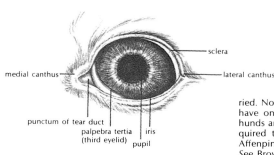

Fig. 109 Eye anatomy

Fig. 110 Eyebrows

ried. Norwich and Norfolk Terriers, for example, have only slight eyebrows; Wire-haired Dachshunds and the Bouvier des Flandres, etc., are required to have bushy eyebrows; those of the Affenpinscher should be shaggy and bristly, etc. See Brows, **Figures 33** and **108**

EYE COLOUR This is directly related to the presence and distribution of the pigment melanin in the iris. The greater this concentration, the darker the eye colour. Most breed standards demand eye colours grading from brown to dark brown. In such cases the amount of melanin is large and its distribution is even. As melanin concentration lessens, the eye colour lightens, eventually to encroach into the amber and gooseberry ranges. Size of pupil also affects eye colour at a given time. In conditions of bright, intense light, the iris contracts. This decreases pupillary size and exposes a large amount of iris to the viewer; hence, true colour is easily seen **(Figure 111)**. Conversely, in poor light the iris pulls back to enlarge the pupil in an attempt to permit the entrance of more light rays. (See **Figure 118**) The

Fig. 111 Eye colour: bird of prey or hawk eyes

larger the pupil, the less the amount of iris exposed and the darker the eye appears, hence the difficulty in discerning a dog's true eye colour in fading or under artificial light.
See Eye Anatomy

Bird of prey eyes Amber- to yellowish-coloured eyes, usually harsh, hard and staring in outlook. Sometimes also referred to as 'hawk eyes', an apt description. Mentioned as a fault, for example, in the breed standard of the German Short-haired Pointer (A.K.C.) **(Figure 111)**.

China eye
See Eye Colour: Wall eye

Fish eye
See Eye Colour: Wall eye

Glass eye Listed as a fault in the A.K.C. version of the Dachshund breed standard; a synonym of china or wall eye.

Gooseberry-coloured eyes Light hazel-coloured eyes with a greenish tint. Listed as a fault in the Curly-Coated Retriever breed standard.

Hawk eyes
See Eye Colour: Bird of prey eyes

Jewelled eye
See Eye Colour: Wall eye

Marbled eye
See Eye Colour: Wall eye

Silver eye
See Eye Colour: Wall eye

Wall eye Incomplete, flecked or spotted distribution of melanin deposits upon a blue iris background; also known as china eye, fish eye, jewelled eye, marbled eye or silver eye. Relatively common in breeds carrying the merle colour gene, e.g., Collie, Cardigan Welsh Corgi, etc., this syndrome may occur in either one or both eyes of any given individual **(Figure 112)**.

EYELIDS
See Eye Anatomy

EYELID, THIRD
See Third eyelid

EYE RIMS The upper and lower margins of the eyelids. The eye rims of dogs are of special

Fig. 112 Eye colour: china or blue eyes on Siberian Husky

significance in dog judging. Firstly, unless their contours are congruent with the eyeball surface as well as reasonably tight, abnormal corneal wear and tear is likely to occur, resulting in excessive tear flow (lachrymation), chronic conjunctivitis, corneal scarring, etc. Ectropion (due to loose eye rims) and entropion (due to inturning eye rims) serve as examples of abnormal eye rim development. Secondly, eye rim colour intensity as well as the extent of its distribution are often taken as an indication of pigmentation in general, e.g., Maltese, in which black eye rims are called for. Although most dog breeds are requested to feature darkly pigmented eye rims, there are some notable exceptions, e.g., Spinone Italiano, Weimaraner.
See also Ectropion, Haw Eyes

Complete eye rims A phrase appearing in the Dalmatian breed standard demanding that the colour around both upper and lower eye rims (black in the black-spotted variety, and liver-brown in the liver-spotted variety) be complete. In this breed a break in colour, irrespective of position, is undesirable.

Loose eye rims A consequence of dropping or sagging eyelids.
See Haw

EYE TYPES The names given to types of eyes refer to the shape of the area exposed by the eye rims, i.e., the orbital aperture. The variations in the appearance of canine eyes are immense. Furthermore, comprehension of existing physical differences is sometimes complicated by the extraordinary choice of descriptive words or phrases employed in some breed standards. The most frequently-used terms applied to canine eyes are listed below.
See Eye Anatomy

Almond eyes Basically of oval shape, bluntly pointed at both corners. Typical of the Basenji, German Shepherd Dog, Irish Water Spaniel, Finnish Spitz and Borzoi **(Figure 113)**.

Fig. 113 Almond eyes: Curly Coated Retriever

Beady eyes Small, round and glittering eyes, imparting an expression foreign to the breed in question. Listed under faults in a number of breeds, e.g., Cocker Spaniel.

Bulging eyes
See Eye Types: Protruding eyes

Circular eyes A reference to correct eye shape in the A.K.C.'s Smooth Fox Terrier breed standard.

Deep-set eyes syn. well-sunken eyes. Meaning eyeballs that are well-seated into deep sockets and hence well-recessed into the skull; typified by the Bull Terrier and Chow Chow **(Figure 114)**.
See **Figure 119**

Fig. 114 Deep set eyes: Chow Chow

Eyes set square to skull An expression used in the Boston Terrier breed standard.
See Eye Types: Obliquely placed eyes

Full eyes
See Eye Types: Protruding eyes

Glassy eyes Fixed, blank and uncomprehending expression. Listed as a fault in the Rough Collie breed standard.

Globular eyes Eyes that appear round in shape, somewhat prominent yet not bulging when viewed in profile **(Figure 115)**.

Goggled eyes syn. protruding eyes. Eyes that appear to be bulging or prominent, staring and rolling. Listed as a fault in the American Cocker Spaniel breed standard.

Haw eyes
See Haw **(Figure 116)**.

Obliquely placed eyes syn. Mongolian eyes. In most canine breeds, eye placement is considered

Fig. 115 Full, round or globular eyes: Chihuahua

Fig. 116 Haw eyes: Bloodhound

correct when the eyes' transverse axes, i.e., from corner to corner, bisect the head's longitudinal axis at right angles (90°); in other words, eyes set square to the skull. Eyes with outer corners situated higher up in the skull than their respective inner ones, i.e., the transverse axes of which run obliquely in relation to the skull's longitudinal axis, are termed 'obliquely placed' or 'slanted'. Although requested in some breed standards, e.g., Bull Terrier, Alaskan Malamute, Finnish Spitz and Flat-coated Retriever, obliquely placed eyes are listed as a fault in others, e.g., English Setter. See **Figures 112** and **114**

Oblong eyes An elliptical eyelid aperture appreciably longer than high, with contours and corners gently rounded rather than angular.

Oval eyes Probably the most common eye shape requested of dogs, e.g., Dachshund, Bouvier des Flandres. Mostly used synonymously with oblong eyes **(Figure 117)**.

Overhung eyes Eyebrows, or superciliary arches, developed to excess, causing such an eye to appear smaller than desired **(Figure 114)**.

Pig eyes Mentioned under faults in A.K.C.'s Miniature Pinscher breed standard, and defined as 'eyes both too small and set too close to one another'.

Prominent eyes
See Eye Types: Protruding eyes

Protruding eyes syn. bulging eyes, full eyes, goggled eyes, prominent eyes. All of these de-

Fig. 117 Oval eyes

scriptive terms probably refer to similar properties in varying degrees of severity, i.e., in the sequence of full to prominent to bulging, and, finally, to protruding. Such eyes are faulty, irrespective of the breed in which they occur. Set prominently in the skull, they are prone to injury and even to prolapse. Apart from such obvious anatomical causes as abnormally large eyeballs and/or shallow sockets, disease such as hyperthyroidism or glaucoma may be responsible for the development of bulgy-eyed appearance **(Figure 118)**.

Receding eyes Eyes deeply positioned in the skull due to eye sockets being too deep or orbs too small or insufficiently well cushioned by orbital muscles and fat.

Fig. 118 Round, protruding, goggling or bulging eyes: Griffon Brabacon

Ringed eyes Eyes exhibiting an abnormal amount of clearly visible sclera surround. A fault listed in the Cairn Terrier breed standard (A.K.C.). See Eye Anatomy

Round eyes Eyes set in circular-shaped apertures, typified by the Griffon Bruxellois, French Bulldog, and American Cocker Spaniel **(Figure 115)**.

Triangular eyes Similar in most respects to oval or oblong eyes, but more angular in contours, e.g., Afghan Hound, Bull Terrier **(Figure 119)**.

Fig. 119 Triangular, deep set eye: Afghan Hound

Well sunken eyes
See Eye Types: Deep set eyes

F

FACE The front part of the head, i.e., the combination of nose, eyes, mouth, cheeks and lips, in common usage often synonymous with foreface.

FACE TYPES

Broken up face A term used to describe the appearance created in a relatively short, wide (brachycephalic) head, as a result of a pushed-in or receding nose surrounded by a well-arched forehead, pronounced stop, undershot jaw, plus deep, well-developed wrinkles. Typified by the British Bulldog and Pekingese **(Figure 120)**.

Fig. 120 Broken-up face, padding: British Bulldog

Clown face Black/white and tan/white markings, more or less symmetrically divided by a longitudinal line down the centre of the skull and foreface. A common occurrence in the Fox Terrier and Bull Terrier **(Figure 121)**.
See **Figure 53**

Fig. 121 Clown face: Fox Terrier (Smooth)

Dish face syn. dished face. Concave contours of the foreface in profile, i.e., converging foreface and skull planes with the tip of the nose at a higher level than the base of the stop. A requirement of the Pointer breed standard; mentioned as faulty construction in the German Short-haired Pointer **(Figure 122)**.
See **Figures 177, 180 and 295**

Fig. 122 Dish face: Pointer

Down-faced syn. hog-faced. By strict definition, foreface and skull planes that diverge, i.e., incline downwards, away from those of the skull. Also used to describe a foreface that curves downwards from the stop to the tip of the nose, i.e., the tip of the nose is below the level of the stop, e.g., Bull Terrier **(Figure 123a)**

Filled-up face Clean, smooth facial contours without excessive muscular development, bony ridges and/or depressions, e.g., Bull Terrier. Also employed in place of 'well-cushioned', especially in short-faced (brachycephalic) breeds **(Figure 123a)**.

Fig. 123a Down or filled-up face (ram's head): Bull Terrier

Frog face Two common, and, to a degree, confusing definitions exist. (a) In reference to the somewhat unusual expression of the Rottweiler, caused by this breed's rather wide mouth and lips that gradually fall away from their centre towards the corners. (b) Faulty facial construction in brachycephalic breeds, especially the British Bulldog, in which the nose extends too far forwards. The original reference dates back to the distinctive differences in the heads of the British Bulldog on the one hand and the French Bulldog on the other **(Figure 123b)**. British Bulldogs resembling the French variety came to be known as 'frog-faced' because of the description of the French as 'Frogs' or 'Froggies'.

Fig. 123b Frog face on French Bulldog (left) and British Bulldog (right)

FAKING The act of disguising or hiding undesirable physical features in show dogs. Examples include coat dyeing, surgical correction of tail or ear carriage, etc.

FALL; FALL OF HAIR
See Hair, Fall of

FANG syn. canine teeth.
See Dentition

FEATHER; FEATHERING syn. flag, fringe, fringing, plume. These terms apply variously to longish coat on the ears, belly, back of legs and tail of many breeds, e.g., English Setter, Gordon Setter, Skye Terrier, Papillon, Clumber Spaniel, etc. On some breeds the name 'fringe' applies more specifically to long hair on the ears, e.g., Dandie Dinmont **(Figure 124)**.
See **Figure 35**

Fig. 124 Feather, flat: English Setter

FEET ANATOMY The feet of dogs are made up of four separate toes or digits, each of which, in turn, consists of three phalanges. The toenails, or claws, arise from the lowest phalanx of each toe. Each toe is joined to its neighbouring partner by tissue, mainly consisting of skin, termed webbing. The extent and development of such webbing varies with the breed. The actual shapes of individual toes, as well as their relationship with associated partners, receive detailed attention in many breed standards. Various descriptions, words and phrases are used, such as: arched, knuckled-up, well split-up, tightly knit, close cupped, etc.

On its bottom and ventral surface, each toe is cushioned by a digital pad. Situated at the rear of the four individual digital pads lies the large metacarpal or communal pad. Structurally, all pads are formed of fatty tissue, interlaced with tough elastic fibres. Their covering is thick, rough and, in most instances, heavily pigmented. Feet and toes with well-developed pads are referred to as 'well-cushioned', 'well-padded', etc. **(Figure 125)**. The front feet of dogs are almost invariably both bigger and broader than the respective hind feet. In all other respects they are identical.
See Feet Types: Webbed feet, Toe Types and Dewclaws

FEET TYPES From all the information available, it appears to be generally accepted that the normal canine foot, i.e., that of feral and domestic dogs, as well as that of their ancestors, is or was either round or slightly oval in shape. This is also the general shape requested by the majority of breed standards. However, numerous variations do exist.

Cat feet Round, compact foot with well-arched toes, tightly bunched or close-cupped, the two centre toes being only slightly longer than those on the outside or inside. The toe pads should be deeply cushioned and covered with thick skin. The impression left by such a foot is round, in contrast to oval. Most breed standards describe cat feet simply state just that, e.g., Boxer, Miniature Pinscher. Others, somewhat surprisingly, adopt unusual verbiage in description, e.g., round feet (Curly-Coated Retriever), circular feet (Sussex Spaniel), close-cupped (Pyrenean Mountain Dog), etc. **(Figures 126a and 126b)**.

Circular feet
See Feet Types: Cat feet

Close-cupped feet
See Feet Types: Cat feet

Compact feet
See Feet Types: Cat feet

Corny feet Feet with soles affected by hard, horny and calloused growths.

East-west feet Front feet, the toes of which turn

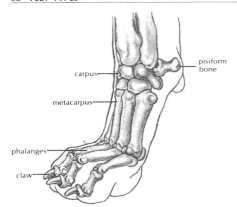

Anatomy of the foot

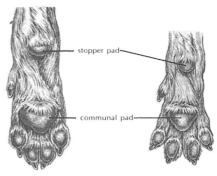

Fig. 126b Well-knit foot (normal construction) (left) compared to splay foot (right) both seen from below

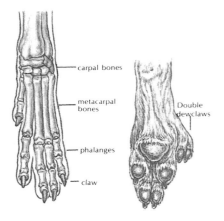

Fig. 125 Feet anatomy and types

Fig. 127 Flat foot, down in pasterns

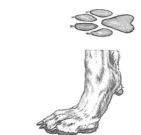

Fig. 128 Hare foot

Fig. 126a Round, cat, circular or compact foot

outwards, away from the centre line; often associated with narrow fronts and/or chests of inadequate depths.
See **Figure 143**

Ferrety feet Long, narrow and flattish feet with toes insufficiently well knuckled-up and poorly cushioned toe pads, similar to hare feet **(Figure 128)** but with flatter toes.

Flat feet Featuring toes which, instead of being well arched, are straight or flat when viewed in profile **(Figure 127)**.

Hare feet syn. rabbit paws. A type in which both centre toes are appreciably longer than the associated outer and inner ones; furthermore, toe arching is less marked, making such feet appear longer overall. Typical of the Borzoi, Chesapeake Bay Retriever, etc. **(Figure 128)**.

Oval feet syn. spoon-shaped feet (German Short-haired Pointer standard). Similar in all respects to cat feet except that both centre toes are slightly longer. As might be expected, such a foot leaves an oval impression on the ground, e.g., Pembroke Welsh Corgi, Pointer **(Figure 129)**.

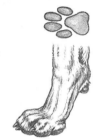

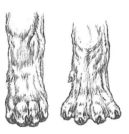

Fig. 130 Well-knit foot (left) compared to splay foot (right): front view

Fig. 129 Oval, spoon-shaped foot

Paper feet Thin and poorly cushioned pads. Similar to ferrety feet, but not necessarily as narrow.

Round feet
See Feet Types: Cat feet

Semi-hare feet These occupy a central position between oval feet on the one hand and hare feet on the other.

Snowshoe feet The specialised feet of the Arctic breeds, i.e., oval, firm, and compact, with well-knit, well-arched toes and tough, deeply cushioned pads. The webbing between the toes is strongly developed and the feet are well furred, even between the toes, as a protection whilst hauling heavy loads for long distances over rough, icy terrain.

Splay feet syn. spread or spreading feet. Feet, irrespective of shape, with toes set rather far apart from one another, i.e., not tightly knit. The term 'splayed' is normally applied to indicate a defect. However, a less marked degree of splay-footedness, due to separation or spreading of the toes, is a desirable feature in some breeds, e.g., Irish Water Spaniel **(Figure 130)**.

Spoon-shaped feet
See Feet Types: Oval feet

Spreading feet
See Feet Types: Splay feet

Webbed feet Typical of water-retrieving breeds, e.g., Newfoundland and Chesapeake Bay Retriever, which, for swimming purposes, require well-developed and strong webbing between the toes; also of Arctic breeds such as the Siberian Husky and Alaskan Malamute, which are required to work in the snow **(Figure 131)**.

Fig. 131 Webbed toes: snow-shoe feet

Well split-up toes
See Toes, Well split-up

FEMUR syn. thigh bone. The longest single bone in the body. Extending from hip to stifle, it forms the bony support of the upper thigh region.
See Hindquarters, **Figure 181**

FERRETY FEET
See Feet Types: Ferrety feet

FETLOCK Adapted from horse terminology, and when applied to dogs, refers to the pastern region, e.g., in the Irish Wolfhound breed standard 'overbent fetlocks' are listed as a fault. In all probability this is a reference to a slope of pastern greater than the ideal, or a pastern too upright.

FIBULA The smaller member of the tibia/fibula combination supporting the lower thigh region. See Hindquarters, **Figure 181**

FIDDLE FRONT
See Front Types: Fiddle front

FILBERT-SHAPED EARS
See Ear Types: Filbert-shaped ears

FILLED-UP FACE
See Face

FINS A colloquial term for too profuse an arrangement of hair on the feet of the Long-haired Dachshund.

FISH EYES
See Eye Colour

FLAG
See Feather

FLAGPOLE TAIL
See Tail Types

FLANK The fleshy portion on the lower border of the couplings region, i.e., the fleshy area near the junction of abdominal floor and hindquarters.
See **Figures 1 and 11**

FLANKS, DRAWN-UP syn. tucked-up flanks. Used in the A.K.C.'s Rottweiler breed standard's list of faults.
See **Figure 356**

FLANKS, TUCKED-UP or TUCKED-IN
See Tuck-up

FLARED NOSTRILS
See Nostrils, flared

FLASHINGS The name given collectively to white markings on the chest, neck, face, feet or tail tip of the Cardigan Welsh Corgi (A.K.C. breed standard) **(Figure 132)**.

Fig. 132 Flashings: Cardigan Corgi

FLAT BACK
See Back Types: Flat back

FLAT CHESTED
See Flat Ribbed

FLAT FEET or FOOTED
See Feet Types: Flat feet

FLAT RIBBED A reference to a chest shape, in cross-section, in which the centre portion of the rib is flattened rather than rounded, e.g., Bedlington Terrier. Whilst usually considered less than desirable, flat ribs are requested by some breed standards, e.g., Bearded Collie.
See Slabsided, Ribs, Chest Capacity, Spring of Ribs, **Figure 273a**

FLECKS; FLECKING Basically spots or spotting. Used in reference to (a) small coat markings of irregular shape, more widely spaced as compared with speckling, and synonymous with ticking,

Fig. 133 Speckled, flecked, ticked or spotted: German Short-haired Pointer

e.g., English Setter and various Pointer breeds **(Figure 133;** See **Figure 35)**, or (b) eyes with blue or black spots on a brown iridal background and/or black spotting on a blue iris, e.g., wall eye.

FLESH, HARD Well developed, strong muscles, denoting top physical condition.

FLESH-COLOURED NOSE
See Nose Types

FLESH MARKS Poorly coloured or unpigmented areas on an otherwise correctly coloured nose, e.g., listed as a fault in the Cavalier King Charles Spaniel breed standard. Flesh marks joining into one another make up into a butterfly nose.
See Nose Types, **Figure 242**

FLESH NOSE syn. flesh-coloured nose.
See Nose Types

FLESHY EARS
See Ear Types

FLEWS The fleshy, sometimes pendulous, upper lips of some breeds, e.g., Bloodhound or Bulldog. Used synonymously for 'lips' in many breed standards **(Figure 134)**.
See **Figures 49b, 57, 203** and **290**

Fig. 134 Flews: Beagle

Flews, tight syn. tight lips.
See Jaws, Tight-lipped

FLEXION The closing or shutting of a joint, in opposition to extension, which opens or straightens a flexed joint.

FLUFFIES Colloquialism for a long-coated variety of the Pembroke Welsh Corgi. An undesirable feature, fluffiness is of genetic origin.

FLUTE; FLUTING
See Median Line

FLUTTERING LIPS
See Lips

FLY or **FLYING EARS**
See Ear Types

FOLDED EARS
See Ear Types

FOOT PADS
See Feet Anatomy

FOREARM syn. lower arm. That area of the forequarters lying between the elbow above and the wrist below: comprised of two parallel long bones, i.e., radius and ulna plus supporting muscles, tendons, etc.
See Forequarters and **Figure 18**

Forearm, turn of Bulldog specialist terminology referring to the pad of muscle on the outside of the foreleg, particularly well-developed near the elbow and tapering down to the wrist **(Figure 135)**.

Fig. 135 Turn of forearm: British Bulldog

FOREFACE That portion of the skull in front of the brain case; also referred to as the muzzle.
See Skull, Face, Muzzle

Foreface, dished
See Face, Dished

Foreface, snipy Basically, a foreface lacking in strength, often due to a combination of weak bone coupled with poor muscle development, frequently accentuated by marked chiselling.

Snipiness is measured in two dimensions, i.e., viewed from above and in profile.
See Muzzle and **Figure 56**

FOREHAND Adapted from horse terminology, meaning the forequarters from the shoulder blades down to the feet.

FORELEG
See Forequarters

Forelegs moving parallel Free, unrestricted movement without weave, paddle, toeing-in, etc. An example is the West Highland White breed standard.
See Gait, **Figure 152**

FOREQUARTERS syn. forelegs, forelimbs, thoracic limbs. The combined front assembly from its uppermost component, the shoulder blade, right down to the feet **(Figure 136)**. The shoulder

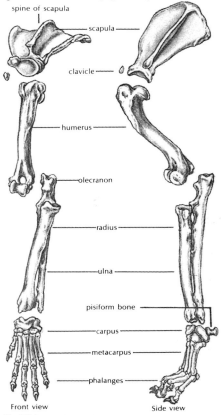

spine of scapula
scapula
clavicle
humerus
olecranon
radius
ulna
pisiform bone
carpus
metacarpus
phalanges

Front view   Side view

Fig. 136 Forequarters anatomy

blade is a relatively large, flat, triangular bone, its highest part, the base, lying just a short distance below the levels of the first and second thoracic vertebral spines; with these it forms the withers region. On its inner surface, the shoulder blade is attached by means of muscles and ligaments to the sides of the first five ribs and adjacent thoracic vertebrae. As there is no bony connection between shoulder blade and chest wall, strong muscular development in this region is absolutely essential; without it, movement tends to suffer, shoulders become loose, backs become soft, etc. The scapula's outer surface is divided approximately in half by a prominent spine which, when palpated (a relatively simple procedure) gives good indication of the so-called 'angulation', 'lay' or 'slope' of shoulders. At the lower end of the shoulder blade there is a shallow depression, the glenoid cavity. The head of the humerus fits snugly into this cavity to form the shoulder joint **(Figure 137)**.

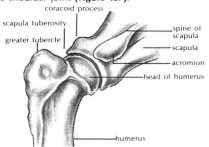

Fig. 137 Point of shoulder: articulation of scapula with humerus

The humerus or arm, the largest bone of the forequarters, lies below the scapula. It is fairly straight and very strong. The angle formed by the scapula/humerus articulation is referred to as the 'forequarters angulation'. This is a most important factor in movement (and therefore of great interest to dog judges). From its shoulder joint articulation, the shaft of the humerus runs in a downwards and backwards direction to end in articulation with the radius and ulna at the elbow joint. These two bones are fused along their length and run almost vertically downwards to the carpus (syn. carpal joint or wrist), forming the forearm region (syn. lower arm). The radius, situated in front, is the larger and main weight-bearing member of the pair. The ulna, both smaller and slimmer, is situated behind the radius and joined firmly to it, so that the two bones move and act as one. At its top section, the ulna flares out to form the olecranon process at the back of the elbow joint, generally identified as the 'point of the elbow'.

The forearm ends at the carpus. The equivalent of man's wrist, this joint consists of seven carpal bones arranged in two transverse rows, plus a series of associated small 'pulley'-type accessory bones. The region between the carpus and the foot is the metacarpus or pastern. It is composed of five relatively slender metacarpal bones. The innermost first metacarpal bone or dewclaw is usually by far the shortest. On rare occasions, however, it is developed to a highly functional and specialised degree, as in the Norwegian Lundehund or Puffin Dog. The final forequarters component is the foot or paw, similar to the hind foot in all respects.
See Angulation, Feet Anatomy

FOREQUARTERS ANGULATION
See Angulation, Forequarters

FOREPAW The forefoot components from the wrist downwards, i.e., the combination of the wrist, pastern and front foot.
See Feet Anatomy

FOXY An adjective found in numerous breed standards. Meaning fox-like, it appears most frequently in the description of head shapes and/or expression, e.g., Pembroke Welsh Corgi, Norwich Terrier, and Finnish Spitz **(Figure 138)**. However, it finds use also in more general terms, e.g., 'fox-like brush' (Cardigan Welsh Corgi), 'general foxy appearance' (Cairn Terrier).
See Tail Types

Fig. 138 Foxy or fox-like head: Finnish Spitz

FREE ACTION
See Action

FRENCH FRONT
See Front Types: French front

FRILL A raised ridge of long or short hair (according to breed), formed by the junction of the mane above and the apron below, extending down the sides of the neck from the base of the ear towards the prosternum. In long-coated dogs the lower portion is sometimes known as the chest frill, e.g., Shetland Sheepdog **(Figure 139)**.
See Figure 17

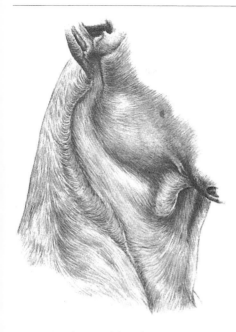

Fig. 139 Frill on short-coated dog: Whippet

FRINGE; FRINGING Synonymous with feather, this is the collection of long hair on the tail, belly and chest, for example, in breeds such as the Gordon Setter, Irish Setter, etc., also on ear fringes, e.g., Skye Terrier, Papillon, Bedlington Terrier **(Figure 140)**.
See **Figures 35, 90** and **124**

FROG FACE
See Face

Fig. 140 Ear fringing, furnishings or feather: Skye Terrier

FRONT TYPES Although technically the word 'front' includes all the components of the forequarter assembly, either singly or in combination, in practice it is generally used to describe that portion from the elbows to the feet as viewed front on. Numerous types of fronts are mentioned in the breed standards.

Bowed front Forearms which, when seen from the front, curve outwards from the elbows then inwards near the wrists. Such an anatomical conformation is generally considered to be faulty, major breed exceptions being the Pekingese and Tibetan Spaniel. A bowed front may be brought about by selection on a genetic basis, nutritional imbalance and/or disease **(Figure 144)**.

Cabriole front
See Fiddle front

Chippendale front
See Fiddle front

Crooked front A reference to the forequarters of some short-legged (achondroplastic) breeds, e.g., Basset Hound, Dachshund, etc., the forearms of which, when viewed head on, incline symmetrically inwards, and are at times slightly curved from the elbows to the wrists. The crooked shape provides a firm cradle-like support for the forward chest portion. In the Dachshund such a front is referred to as the 'crook'.
See Crook, **Figure 68**

East-west front Incorrectly positioned pasterns that cause the feet to turn outwards, away from the centre line. Usually associated with a narrow front **(Figure 143)**.

Fiddle front syn. cabriole front, Chippendale front. A front assembly which, from front on, resembles a fiddle or violin shape, i.e., the elbows rather wide apart, forearms sloping in towards the centre, with pasterns and feet turning out **(Figure 147)**.

French front A narrow front with pasterns angled out, resembling the position assumed by a French dancing master **(Figure 143)**.

Gun barrel front Synonym for a 'true' or straight front when viewed head on. The forearms and pasterns are straight, positioned vertically to the ground and parallel to each other **(Figure 141)**.

Horseshoe front When seen front on, one showing straight forearms, yet further apart at the elbows than at the wrists, i.e., inclined inwards, but with pasterns perpendicular to the ground. Typical of the Bedlington Terrier **(Figures 148a and 148b)**.

Narrow front Usually taken as a front in which the forearms, when seen head on, stand closer to one another than desirable. Although mostly assumed to be an anatomical defect, especially in working breeds, due to its action on the heart and lung capacity plus adverse effect on gait, some breed standards, e.g., Borzoi and Irish Setter, call for relatively narrow fronts (the emphasis here being on the word relative), yet compensate for possible loss of chest capacity by demanding maximum depth **(Figure 145)**.

Pigeon-toed front Pasterns and feet turning inwards towards the midline. The opposite to an 'east-west' front **(Figure 142)**.

Pinched front syn. narrow front. Used in the A.K.C.'s Miniature Schnauzer breed standard to describe a fault.

Steep front Forequarters in which the shoulder blade/humerus angle, observed side on, is greater than ideal, i.e., a steeper or more upright shoulder placement than preferred.

See Angulation, **Figure 14**, Shoulders, Steep in, **Figure 289**

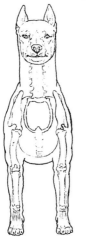
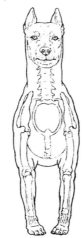

Fig. 141 Normal, straight, gun-barrel front

Fig. 142 Pigeon-toed front

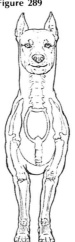
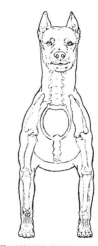

Fig. 145 Narrow front

Fig. 146 Wide front

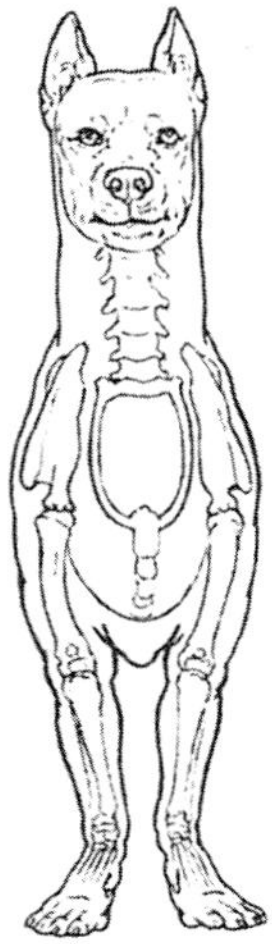

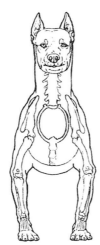

Fig. 143 East-west feet: French front

Fig. 144 Bandy, bowed or out in elbows front

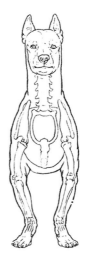

Fig. 147 Chippendale, fiddle or cabriole front

Straight front syn. gun barrel front, true front. In normal canine anatomy, a dog's front, viewed head on, features forearms that run perpendicular to the ground as well as parallel to each other. This structural formation continues from the elbows, through the wrists and pasterns right down to the feet. Such a front is called straight and true **(Figure 141)**.

FRONTAL BONES Major skull components, responsible to a large extent for the formation and shape of the forehead, e.g., 'frontal bones very slightly raised' (Irish Wolfhound breed standard). In other breeds, e.g., Newfoundland, Pointer, they are pronounced **(Figure 149)**.
See **Figure 177**

Fig. 149 Frontal bones: Newfoundland

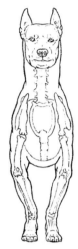

Fig. 148a Horseshoe front (faulty)

Fig. 148b Horseshoe front: Bedlington Terrier (normal)

True front
See Front Types: Straight front

Wide front A front assembly wider than normally acceptable. Such a front, though considered faulty in some breeds, is permissible, even desirable, in others, e.g., British Bulldog **(Figure 146)**.

FROSTING A process similar to greying at the temples in man, i.e., the gradual replacement of coloured hair by white hair, usually commencing about the face. Although normally associated with advancing age, frosting about the muzzle does occur relatively early in some breeds of dog, e.g., Belgian Tervueren.

FROUFROU Synonym for the tuft of hair (pompom) on the tail tip of some breeds; the result of trimming **(Figure 345)**.

FROWN Worried or concerned expression caused by slight skin wrinkles across the head and above the eyes.
See Brows, Wrinkling, **Figures 94, 99a and 363**

FULL DROP EARS
See Ear Types

FULL EYES
See Eye Types

FURNISHINGS The desirable abundance of coat at the extremities (including head and tail) of some breeds. Many requests for furnishings appear in the breed standards, e.g., the profuse head whiskers of the broken-coated Terrier breeds, the ear fringes of the Afghan Hound, the leg hair of the Setter breeds, the eyebrows of the Schnauzers, the beard of the Griffon Bruxellois, the moustache of the Bouvier des Flandres, etc. When present in the required amount, a dog is said to be 'well-furnished'.
See **Figures 35, 140** and **218**

FURROW
See Median line

G

GAIT syn. action, motion, movement. A most important consideration in dog appraisal, especially the evaluation of working and sporting breeds. Not only are some dog breeds required to move in a characteristic, individualistic fashion, but sound, balanced gait, in all but the rarest instances, also indicates correct physical construction. Anatomically incorrect specimens are rarely, if ever, capable of sound movement.

The basic gaits of dogs are: walk, amble, pace, trot, canter and gallop. All of these, plus some intermediary and/or unusual types, are described briefly below. However, serious students of this subject are referred to Rachel Page Elliott's excellent text *Dogsteps* (Howell Book House Inc.,

New York, U.S.A.), as well as Curtis and Thelma Brown's *The Art and Science of Judging Dogs* (B. & F. Publications Inc., California, U.S.A.). **Figure 150** shows various types of gaits of individual breeds; **Figure 151** illustrates changes in angulation during gaiting.
See Action

Amble A type of gait in which the front and hind legs on the same side move in unison with one another as a pair. The amble is similar to the pace in all respects except that it is slower and that in the latter both feet on the same side hit the ground simultaneously, while in the amble the rear foot of a pair is raised off the ground just a

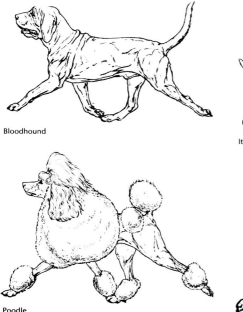

Bloodhound

Poodle

Fig. 150 Gaits of various breeds

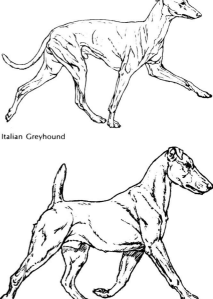

Italian Greyhound

Smooth Fox Terrier

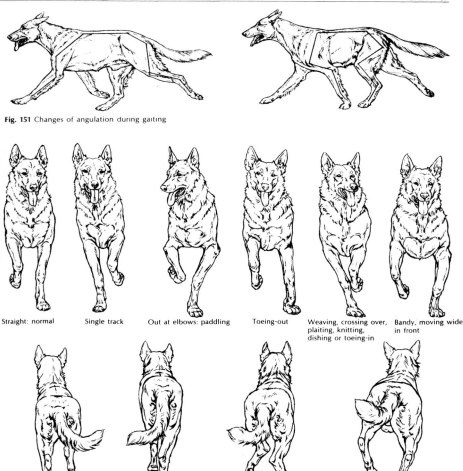

Fig. 151 Changes of angulation during gaiting

Straight: normal   Single track   Out at elbows: paddling   Toeing-out   Weaving, crossing over, plaiting, knitting, dishing or toeing-in   Bandy, moving wide in front

Straight: normal   Close behind   Cow-hocked   Bow-hocked, bandy, moving wide behind

Fig. 152 Gaits as seen from front and rear

fraction sooner than the front member, hence, of necessity, it is also brought into ground contact a little earlier.

Canter Not generally used for describing canine action, the canter is basically a slow form of gallop. Its step sequence resembles the walk but without the same regularity.

Cow-hocked gait Animals affected by cow hocks (i.e., hind legs in which the hocks incline inwards towards each other instead of being parallel) tend to 'brush' the inside edges of their rear pasterns against one another in passing. The result is a gait severely restricted in freedom of movement **(Figure 152)**.

Crabbing Forward movement in which the spinal column is not pointed in the direction of travel, rather, it deviates at an angle so that one rear leg passes on the inside of the front foot, while the other does so on the outside of its partner, instead of travelling in line with them. Called 'sidewinding' by American dog fanciers.

Crossing over An abnormality of gait, seen in either fore- or hindquarter movement and, at times, in both, in which the feet, when extended, cross over in front of one another as well as over an imaginary centre line drawn under the body. There are several causes for this type of action. By far the most common is a chest either insufficiently wide or deep, sometimes both **(Figure 152)**.
See Weaving

Dishing syn. weaving. An abnormal type of forequarter movement mentioned in the Wire Fox Terrier breed standard **(Figure 152)**.

Frictionless gait Free, effortless, easy gait without physical contact between individual members.

Gallop The fastest movement of the dog, the gallop is a four-time gait in which the dog is fully suspended or airborne once during each motion sequence. The actual movement pattern is: right front foot, left front foot, right rear foot, left rear foot. Suspension occurs immediately after taking off from the left front foot. The gallop of the Greyhound differs from that of other dogs in that it consists of a series of gigantic leaps, leaving the animal totally airborne for considerable periods of time. This type of motion is referred to as a double suspension gallop. **Figure 153** compares the gallop of the Greyhound with that of other breeds.

Goose-stepping gait A movement typified by accentuated lift of the forelimbs, similar in most respects to a hackney gait, but coupled with full extension of front pasterns and feet before placing these in contact with the ground, e.g., Japanese Chin **(Figure 154)**.

Hackney gait Characterised by exaggerated lift of pasterns and front feet, also to a degree the hind feet. The term is taken from the hackney horse which exemplifies this action. Although specifically requested in some breed standards, e.g., Miniature Pinscher and Italian Greyhound, hackneying is an abnormal movement that requires rather steep shoulder angulation, coupled with upright pasterns. It tends to waste energy (due to high lift and shortened step), thereby lessening endurance **(Figure 155)**.

Moving close Terminology applied to fore and/or hind limbs that are insufficiently well separated from one another during movement. In extreme cases the legs of animals moving closely, on passing, touch or 'brush' up against one another along their inner borders **(Figure 152)**.

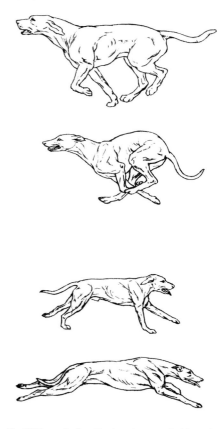

Fig. 153 Types of gallop: Greyhound compared with sporting and working breeds

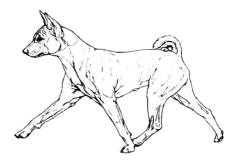

Fig. 154 Goose-stepping Basenji (faulty)

Fig. 155 Hackney gait: Miniature Pinscher (correct)

Fig. 157 Comparison between trot (top) and pace

Fig. 156 Over reaching Pointer (faulty)

Over-reach; over-reaching gait A not uncommon kind of action in dogs, observable in profile and especially when moving fast, in which the hind feet are thrust past their front counterparts (on the outside) before making contact with the ground **(Figure 156)**.

Pace A two-time gait with a pattern of (a) two right feet on the ground and two left feet in the air and (b) two left feet on the ground and two right feet in the air, i.e., both right legs move forwards, simultaneously followed by both left legs. Some dog breeds typically pace when moving at slow speeds (e.g., English Springer Spaniel and Pyrenean Mountain Dog); others when walking or trotting (Old English Sheepdog). **Figures 157 and 158** show the difference between the trot and pace from side, front and back views.

Paddling Incorrect and energy-wasting movement of the forequarters in which pasterns and feet perform circular, exaggerated motion, turning or flicking outwards at the end of each step; may be associated with tied-in shoulders **(Figure 152)**.

Plait; plaiting Crossing-over type of movement of the front legs, sometimes also referred to as 'knitting' **(Figure 152)**.

Side-winding
See Crabbing

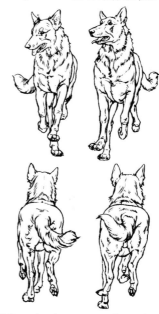

Fig. 158 Comparison between trot and pace: front and rear views

Single tracking In normal canine movement, irrespective of breed (but more readily observed in the taller varieties) the tendency is for the legs to incline more and more under the body as the speed increases. Eventually, the paws, as seen by their imprints, come to travel in a single line. Such action is referred to as single tracking; a not uncommon type of gait sometimes requested of the Otter Hound, Kuvasz and numerous other breeds **(Figure 152)**.

Stilted or **Stilty gait** Hobbled, short-stepping, choppy and/or restricted movement, lacking drive. The opposite to free, reachy or powerful action, a stilted gait is usually the result of inadequate angulation of fore- and/or (especially) hindquarters, at times coupled with lack of proper muscle development. Despite being a hindrance to normal canine activity, a stilted gait is nevertheless required in the Chow Chow.

Toeing-in Forefeet rotated in towards each other and the centre line instead of being in direct continuation with the line of the pastern. 'Toeing-in' may take place when standing, moving or both. It may affect only the feet or involve the pastern also **(Figure 152)**.

Trot Like the pace, the trot is a two-time gait, but of diagonal sequence, i.e., the right front foot and the left hind foot are on the ground at the one time, while the left front foot and right rear foot are in the air. This is followed by the sequence of left front foot and right rear foot on the ground, with the right front and left rear feet in the air. **Figures 157** and **158** show the difference between the trot and pace from front, back and side views.

Walk The least tiring and slowest of all gaits; a four-time gait, i.e., each limb moves one after the other. The sequence is: right front foot, left rear foot, left front foot, right rear foot. Then the cycle is repeated.

Weaving syn. crossing over, dishing, plaiting. Front or hindquarter motion in which the free foot at first swings around the support foot, then forwards and inwards, eventually crossing the latter's path before being set down on the ground. Dishing, as referred to, for example, in the Fox Terrier breed standard, is synonymous with weaving; so is plaiting. Mostly such action is regarded as faulty **(Figure 152)**.

GASKIN A synonym, taken from horse terminology, for the lower or second thigh; used in the Bloodhound breed standard.
See Thigh

GESTATION The process of carrying the young, i.e., pregnancy; in the canine species this lasts approximately sixty-three days (nine weeks).

GIANT BREEDS Classification of dog breeds frequently takes place under the headings of miniature, small, medium-sized and large, ranging from the Chihuahua at one extreme to the Afghan Hound at the other. Using such criteria puts the Great Dane, Mastiff, Pyrenean Mountain Dog, Saint Bernard, Borzoi, Deerhound, Irish Wolfhound, etc., into the so-called 'giant breeds' category, i.e., much larger and/or heavier than the average. The Mastiff is the heaviest breed in existence, averaging 75 kg (165 lb), while the Irish

Fig. 159 Giant breeds: Irish Wolfhound

Wolfhound is the tallest (one is known to have reached 100 cm or 39.5 in) **(Figure 159)**.
See Acromegaly

GIGANTISM
See Acromegaly

GIRTH Measurement of the chest circumference taken at the point of maximum development just behind the withers.
See **Figure 216**

GIVING TONGUE A huntsman's expression for the baying noise or 'music' made by hounds when at work.

GLASS or **GLASSY EYES**
See Eye Types: Glass eye

GLAUCOUS Adjective used in A.K.C.'s version of the Old English Sheepdog breed standard, meaning greyish-blue.

GLOBULAR EYES
See Eye Types: Globular eyes

GOGGLED EYES
See Eye Types: Goggled eyes

GOOSEBERRY EYES
See Eye Types: Gooseberry eyes

GOOSE NECK
See Neck Types

GOOSE RUMP
See Rump

GOOSE-STEPPING GAIT
See Gait

GRIZZLE Normally defined as a blueish-grey or iron-grey colour, due to an admixture of black and white hairs, e.g., Border Terrier and Norfolk Terrier. Reference to red grizzle is made in the Lakeland Terrier breed standard. In this case white pigment is replaced by red pigment. 'Grizzle' is used also to describe the 'widow's peak' pattern on the Saluki.

See **Figure 79**

GUARD HAIRS The longer, stiffer hair, compris-ing the outer jacket and supported by, as well as protecting, the softer, dense undercoat, e.g., German Shepherd Dog, Keeshond. Also referred to in some Canadian breed standards (e.g., Eskimo Dog) as 'master hair'.

See **Figure 61**

GUN BARREL FRONT
See Front Types

H

HACKLES The name given to the outer coat's guard hairs on the neck and back region when raised during fright or anger; basically, a protective mechanism to impress and/or scare away adversaries. The control of the erectile tissue responsible for such 'hackle raising' is involuntary.

HACKNEY GAIT or **ACTION**
See Gait

HAIR, FALL OF A fringe or shock of hair on top of the head, falling forward to cover portion of the face, ears and/or eyes, e.g., Lhasa Apso, Yorkshire Terrier. When such a fall covers the eyes, it is frequently referred to as a 'veil' or 'umbrella' **(Figure 160)**.
See **Figure 64**

Fig. 160 Fall of hair over eyes: Briard

HALLMARKS Physical characteristics, specific to a given breed. Examples include: spectacles in the Keeshond, saddle coat pattern in the Afghan Hound, molero in the Chihuahua, etc.

HALO; HALOES The narrow circular ring of black or very dark skin surrounding the eyes of the Bichon Frisé. The illusion of haloes, enhanced by hair trimming round the eyes, accentuates the eye size, thereby creating this breed's typical expression **(Figure 161)**.

HAM; HAMS Mostly applied to the muscle groupings of the upper thigh, i.e., the region extending from the hip to the stifle. Occasionally,

Fig. 161 Haloes: Bichon Frise

however, e.g., in the Old English Sheepdog breed standard, the word 'hams' is used to include both the upper and lower thighs. Some A.K.C. breed standards substitute 'hams' for 'thighs' when speaking of both upper and lower thighs.
See **Figures 46b** and **307**

HANGING EARS
See Ear Types

HARD-DRIVING ACTION
See Action

HARE A colour often mentioned in Hound breed standards, e.g., Basset Griffon Vendeen.
See Badger

HARE FEET
See Feet Types

HARE LIP
See Lip

HARLEQUIN Normally a reference to the fairly common patched or pied colour pattern in Great Danes, characterised by black and/or blue-grey patches on a white background. For preference such colour patches should be roughly of similar size and have a torn-edged appearance **(Figure 162)**. Ideally the neck and forechest areas should be free of patching. The F.C.I. definition extends the use of 'harlequin' to include black patches on blue-grey animals with white markings, resembling merle, e.g., Norwegian Dunker Stövare.

HAUNCH The muscular development around the haunch bone area, i.e., the most forward region of the croup.

HAUNCH BONES syn. aitches, hip bones. Situated at the front of the pelvic girdle, the haunch

Fig. 162 Harlequin colour pattern: Great Dane

bones are technically the iliac crests of the pelvic wings which serve as anchorage points to the sides of the sacrum.

In some breeds, e.g., Afghan Hound, Saluki, etc., the haunch bones appear as distinct prominences well above the backline **(Figure 163)**. Such placement is usually indicative of steep pelvic slope (on occasions, a similar but less desirable appearance is created by lack of rump muscle development). In contrast, in breeds with relatively flat positioned pelvic girdles, e.g., Gordon Setter, the haunch bones blend almost imperceptibly into the topline. *See* Hindquarters, Spinal column

Fig. 163 Prominent hips or haunch bones: Afghan Hound

HAW; HAW-EYEDNESS syn. ectropion. Drooping, pouching or sagging of the lower eyelid or lids, due to looseness, resulting in the exposure of an abnormally large amount of conjunctival lining. Usually, but not always, such pocketing occurs near the centre of the eyelid margin. A dog so affected is said to be 'haw-eyed', or exhibiting signs of ectropion **(Figure 164)**. In most breeds, the margins of both upper and lower eyelids are required to be relatively tight, snugly fitting the eyeballs' contours. Such arrangement allows for natural unimpeded tear secretion, flow and drainage. Excessive lower eyelid margin laxity not only exposes an area of conjunctival lining normally hidden, it also creates a

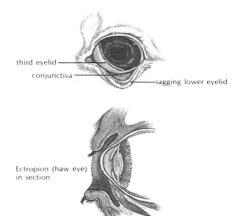

third eyelid — conjunctiva — sagging lower eyelid

Ectropion (haw eye) in section

Fig. 164 Ectropion (haw eye)

Fig. 165 Haw-eyed appearance

pocket for tear pooling and stagnation. In due course this leads to bacterial invasion, followed by the symptoms of chronic conjunctivitis, i.e., inflammation and increased lachrymation (tear flow). Mainly due to genetic influences (it can be brought about by injuries as well), haw-eyedness is considered an undesirable feature in most breed standards **(Figure 165)**. It is, however, a requirement in some, e.g., Bloodhound, Saint Bernard, etc. *See* **Figure 116**

HAWK EYES
See Eye Colour

HEAD The frontmost part of the canine skeleton, joining at its base to the first cervical vertebra (atlas). The term 'head' is generally taken to include all the structures surrounding and incor-

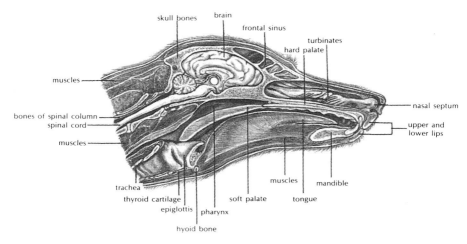

skull bones brain
frontal sinus
turbinates
hard palate
muscles
nasal septum
bones of spinal column
spinal cord
upper and
lower lips
muscles
muscles mandible
trachea
thyroid cartilage soft palate tongue
epiglottis pharynx
hyoid bone

Fig. 166 Cross-section through head

porated within the bony framework of the skull.
Figure 166 shows a cross-section through the
skull in profile.
See Skull

HEAD TYPES
Apple head
See Skull Types: Apple skull **(Figure 167)**

Fig. 167 Apple head: Chihuahua

Fig. 168 Balanced head: Gordon Setter

Balanced head A reference to approximately
equal lengths of skull and foreface; required of
many breed standards, e.g., Gordon Setter,
Afghan Hound **(Figure 168)**.

Blocky head A broader head than that considered
to be ideal.
See Blocky

Brick-shaped head Applies to a relatively long
rectangular head (when viewed from above), i.e.,
one in which the widths of skull and muzzle are
approximately equal, e.g., Fox Terrier (Wire), Basset Hound, the opposite to cone-shaped **(Figure
169)**.

Fig. 169 Rectangular or brick-shaped head: Fox Terrier (Wire)

Clean head A head devoid of extraneous muscular or bony lumps, and/or free of wrinkles **(Figure 172)**.

Coarse head Usually a head broader than ideal, its outline spoiled by excessively lumpy bone and/or muscle development.

See **Figure 43**

Coffin head A long, relatively narrow head, coffin-shaped in outline when viewed front on, occasionally seen in the Borzoi or Collie (Rough).

Cone-shaped or **conical head** A common head shape amongst dogs, e.g., Dachshund, Dobermann. It is triangular in outline, when seen both side on and from above, i.e., conical in shape **(Figure 170)**.

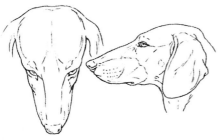

Fig. 170 Cone-shaped head: Dachshund

Egg-shaped head Self-explanatory construction of head, typified by the Bull Terrier **(Figure 171)**.

Fig. 171 Egg-shaped head: Bull Terrier

Fox-like head A common Spitz type of head. Basically of elongated and triangular shape with base appreciably narrower than length, and relatively fine foreface, e.g., Finnish Spitz, Keeshond, Welsh Corgi.

See **Figure 138**

Gaunt head Description used in the breed standards of the Belgian Shepherd Dog (Groenendael) and Hungarian Vizsla. Gaunt, meaning emaciated, abnormally lean, etc., is probably a somewhat incorrect and severe translation intended to be taken as synonymous with clean and dry as used in other breed standards.

Long or **tapering head** Typified by the long, narrow, tapering, V-shaped head of the Collie or Borzoi, usually associated with slight or imperceptible stop **(Figure 172)**.

See Skull Types

Fig. 172 Long or tapering head: Saluki

Otter head Alludes specifically to the head shape of the Border Terrier, which is said to resemble that of an otter **(Figure 173)**.

Border Terrier   Otter

Fig. 173 Otter head

Pear-shaped head Used in the Bedlington Terrier breed standard to describe that breed's head contours **(Figure 174)**.

Ram's head A combination of skull and foreface contours which, when viewed in profile, appear convex, i.e., the top lines of the skull and muzzle incline in diverging directions, the highest point being at the brows, e.g., Bedlington Terrier, Bull Terrier **(Figure 175)**.

Rectangular head Head profile is rectangular in shape, its appearance often enhanced by furnishings, e.g., Wire Fox Terrier **(Figure 169)**.

Short or **round head** One with a muzzle excessively foreshortened and a skull both broad

Fig. 174 Pear-shaped head: Bedlington Terrier

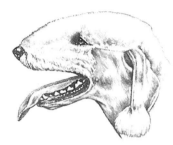

Fig. 175 Ram's head: Bedlington Terrier

Fig. 176 Short, round head: French Bulldog

and square, giving a general impression of round-ness, e.g., French Bulldog **(Figure 176)**.

Squared-off head Refers to muzzle or lip shape, i.e., front squared off, as compared to V-shaped Borzoi or rounded French Bulldog heads **(Figure 177)**.

Fig. 177 Squared-off head: Pointer

Two-angled head Mentioned as a fault in the A.K.C.'s Shetland Sheepdog breed standard, a two-angled head refers to diverging head planes when viewed in profile, in contrast to the desirable parallel head planes of that breed.
See Head Planes, **Figure 180**

Unbalanced head Incorrect, uneven proportions of skull and foreface. For example, the Rough Collie breed standard requests equal lengths of skull and foreface. In this breed, such proportions are required for a balanced head. Any variations from these criteria, i.e., a foreface appreciably longer than skull length or vice versa, would produce an 'unbalanced' head.

V-shaped head
See Head Types: Wedge-shaped head

Wedge-shaped head syn. V-shaped head. One that is triangular or wedge-shaped when viewed either in profile or from above, or both, in which case the wedge shapes need not necessarily be of equal dimensions, thereby differing from a conical head. All kinds of wedge-type head formations occur in dogs, ranging from wide base and short length (Siberian Husky) to narrow base and long length (Collie) **(Figure 178)**.

Fig. 178 Wedge-shaped head: Basset Artesian Normand

HEAD CARRIAGE, LOFTY or **PROUD** Aristocratic bearing, accentuated by a head both set correctly as well as held high on a strong, clean and well-crested neck, e.g., Basenji **(Figure 179)**.

Fig. 179 Lofty head carriage

HEAD PLANES The geometrical contours, viewed in profile, of (a) the top skull, from occiput to stop, and (b) the foreface, i.e., from stop to tip of nose. Usually head planes are spoken of in relation to one another. In the Bouvier des Flandres' breed standard, for example, they are required to be straight and parallel. In the Pointer, on the other hand, these planes tend to converge **(Figure 180)**.

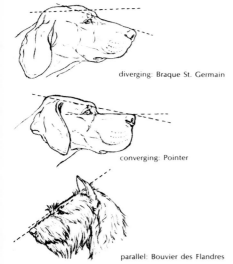

diverging: Braque St. Germain

converging: Pointer

parallel: Bouvier des Flandres

Fig. 180 Head planes

HEART ROOM, PLENTY OF Colloquialism to indicate ample room within the chest cavity, sufficient to allow for maximum heart development and functions. Ample heart room' infers a chest construction in concert with optimum stamina, e.g., English Springer Spaniel.

HEART-SHAPED EARS
See Ear Types

HEEL Equivalent to the hock joint or tarsus. However, according to the wording of some breed standards, it is the lower end of the rear pastern, e.g., the Gordon Setter breed standard says 'hock to heel short and strong'; this terminology is technically incorrect.
See Hindquarters

HEIGHT Correctly measured as the distance from the withers to the ground when the animal is standing normally, i.e., with points of hocks only a short distance out from the rearmost projection of the upper thigh, plus both forearms and rear pasterns at right angles to the ground.
See Measurements, **Figure 216**

HIGH IN STATION; HIGH STATIONED
See Station

HIGH IN WITHERS
See Withers, High in

HIGH ON LEG
See Leggy

HINDQUARTERS syn. quarters, pelvic limb **(Figure 181)**. These commence with the pelvic girdle, consisting of two fused halves attached to the sides of the sacral vertebrae of the spinal column **(Figure 182)**. Composed of three bones, the ilium, ischium and pubis, each pelvic half, when viewed side on, exhibits an iliac wing in front and an ischiac tuber at the rear. Approximately halfway between these two landmarks but at a slightly lower level (at the fusion point of these two bones) lies the acetabulum or hip socket. Into this fits the head of the femur or thigh bone, the longest single bone in the skeleton. The angle formed between a straight line drawn through the iliac wing and ischial tuber and the horizontal determines the pelvic slope. The angle formed by the identical line with the femur's longitudinal axis is the pelvic angle.

The femur runs downwards and forwards to end in articulation with the tibia and fibula at the stifle joint. The muscle groupings surrounding the femur form the thigh or upper thigh region. At the front of its lower end the femur forms a shallow groove (trochlea) in which lies the kneecap or patella, firmly anchored by a series of ligaments.

The stifle or knee joint is made up of the lower end of the femur, the kneecap and the upper

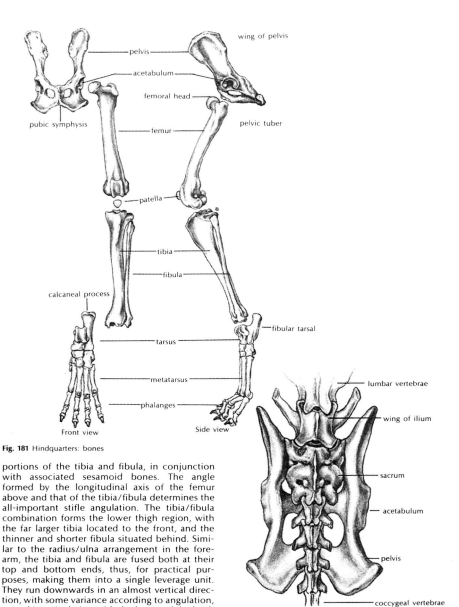

pelvis

wing of pelvis

acetabulum

femoral head

pubic symphysis

pelvic tuber

femur

patella

tibia

fibula

calcaneal process

fibular tarsal

tarsus

metatarsus

lumbar vertebrae

phalanges

wing of ilium

Front view

Side view

Fig. 181 Hindquarters: bones

sacrum

acetabulum

pelvis

coccygeal vertebrae

portions of the tibia and fibula, in conjunction with associated sesamoid bones. The angle formed by the longitudinal axis of the femur above and that of the tibia/fibula determines the all-important stifle angulation. The tibia/fibula combination forms the lower thigh region, with the far larger tibia located to the front, and the thinner and shorter fibula situated behind. Similar to the radius/ulna arrangement in the forearm, the tibia and fibula are fused both at their top and bottom ends, thus, for practical purposes, making them into a single leverage unit. They run downwards in an almost vertical direction, with some variance according to angulation, to end in articulation with the bones of the hock joint or tarsus.

Fig. 182 Pelvic girdle seen from above

The tarsus or heel consists of seven tarsal bones. The largest of these, the fibular tarsal, is situated at the rear. Its uppermost process, the calcaneus, serves as an anchorage point for the Achilles tendon insertion, this area being referred to as the point of the hock, i.e., equivalent to the heel of man.

Four metatarsal bones are situated beneath the tarsus. Combined, they form the metatarsus or rear pastern, resembling the corresponding metacarpal bones of the fore limb in general form They are, however, slightly longer. The first metatarsal bone is often absent, but, when present, it forms the rear dewclaw, situated on the inner surface of each hind leg. The hind feet are similar to the forepaws in all respects, except that, usually, they are both smaller and longer as well as narrower.

See **Figures 6, 187** and **305**

Angulation of hindquarters
See Angulation

Drooping hindquarters The appearance in profile imparted by a steeply sloping, relatively long pelvic girdle, i.e., haunch bones appreciably higher than the pelvic tuber. Typical of the Deerhound and Irish Wolfhound.

See Crouch, Droop, **Figure 80**

Hindquarters chopped off behind syn. quarters chopped off behind. Unusual terminology employed in the Foxhound breed standard for buttocks and rear upper thigh edges which fail to extend past the set-on of the tail. Obviously, such hindquarters would be incapable of generating the desired power and drive required in this breed. Anatomically, the reason for this kind of faulty construction is usually a combination of very short and steeply set pelvis, coupled with narrow thigh muscles **(Figure 183)**.

Fig. 183 Hindquarters chopped off behind

Hindquarters too far back
See Hindquarters too far under

Hindquarters too far under In the vast majority of breeds, the so-called 'normal stance' is adopted when an animal's forearms are placed perpendicular to the ground, with rear pasterns similarly positioned, and the point of the hock some 3 cm to 5 cm behind the rearmost projection of the upper thigh. Most backlines, under these circumstances, are level from end of withers to loins; some slope down slightly, whilst a few, e.g., Old English Sheepdog, slope upwards to the rear. Dogs standing with their hocks more directly under the body than desirable, often accompanied by sloping rear pasterns, may be referred to as having hindquarters positioned too far under **(Figure 184)**. Conversely, dogs with hocks and rear pasterns placed further back than ideal are said to have hindquarters standing too far back **(Figure 185)**.

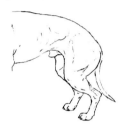

Fig. 184 Hindquarters too far under

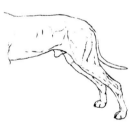

Fig. 185 Hindquarters too far back

Light in hindquarters syn. racy or rangy hindquarters. A phrase with two meanings: (a) slim, streamlined or slender hindquarters construction as required for a particular breed, e.g., Staffordshire Bull Terrier, (b) hindquarter muscle development lighter or less than ideal.

See **Figures 270** and **271**

Racy hindquarters
See Light in hindquarters

HIP; HIPS Technically, the hip joint, i.e., the articulation between the femoral head and the pelvic acetabulum. More generally used in reference to the so-called hip or haunch bones or the general area around the junction of the upper thigh and rump regions.

See Hindquarters, Haunch bones

HIP BONES
See Haunch bones

HIP DYSPLASIA A developmental disease of the canine hip joint, occurring primarily in larger breeds. It is caused by (a) increased joint laxity (b) abnormal contours of one or both hip joint components, or a combination of (a) and (b). Whatever the cause or causes, the result is excessive wear and tear within a normally congruous ball-and-socket joint. In time this leads to joint remodelling as well as to the deposition of arthritic tissue. Symptoms vary from mild, transient lameness to permanent crippling in severely affected cases. Whilst most experts hold this disease to be of genetic origin, its mode of inheritance is as yet not firmly established; however, it is thought that both nutritional and environmental factors play some part in its origin. **Figure 186a** shows head of femur displacement in two grades of hip dysplasia; these can be compared with the normal position in **Figure 186b**. The latter also shows the position of the pectineus muscle which is sometimes severed surgically in the hope that such operation will offer some relief from joint pain.

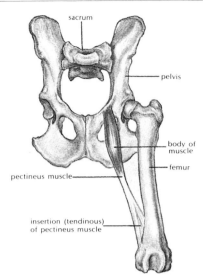

Fig. 186b Position of pectineus muscle: normal hip joint

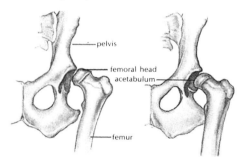

Fig. 186a Two grades of hip dysplasia: severe (left) and mild

HIP JOINT
See Hindquarters, Acetabulum

HIP SOCKET
See Hindquarters

HIPS, PROMINENT or **PROMINENT IN** Haunch bones set on a level higher than that of the corresponding dorsal vertebral spines, not infrequently rather sparingly covered with muscle, thus appearing prominent to the observer. Such construction usually denotes a steep lay of pelvis and is typical of many hound and hunting breeds, e.g., Afghan Hound, Saint Germain Pointer. *See* Haunch, **Figure 163**

HOCK, HOCK JOINT A joint on the hind limb, located between the lower thigh and rear pastern

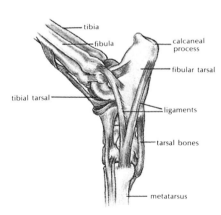

Fig. 187 Hock joint, showing ligaments

(Figure 187). In lay terminology the word 'hock' usually relates to the calcaneus or 'point of hock' situated at the rear of the hock joint. Not infrequently, breed standard descriptions tend to use 'hock' as synonymous with the rear pastern as a whole. This usage accounts for phrases such as 'short in hock', 'long in hock', etc., all of which are technically incorrect.
See Hindquarters

HOCK TYPES (Figures 188a, 188b and **188c)**
Barrel hocks syn. bow hocks.
Bow hocks syn. barrel hocks.
See Cow hocks

Cow hocks In a soundly constructed dog, standing naturally and viewed from the rear, an imaginary plumb line drawn through the pelvic tubers should bisect both the upper and lower thighs, pass through the point of the hock, and then continue along the centre of the rear pastern into the foot. A hock turning inwards from such a line, depending upon the degree, may be taken as 'cow-hocked' Conversely, outwards turning of the hocks is referred to as 'bow-hocked' or 'barrel-hocked'. Both conditions represent anatomical abnormalities and unsoundness. Cow hocks produce restricted action, lacking freedom of movement, with the rear pasterns tending to 'brush' against one another when passing. Animals affected by bow hocks, on the other hand, appear to stand wide behind and move with a waddle.
See Gait and **Figure 272**

High or **High in hocks** Undesirable construction, due to metatarsi or rear pasterns longer than ideal, or to insufficient slope of rear pastern for a particular breed. Either condition tends to render the distance between the point of the hock and the ground greater than desired for that breed.

Hocks close to the ground A requirement of the Kerry Blue Terrier breed standard.
See Well let down hocks

Hocks square with body Hock points positioned in line with the rearmost edge of the upper thigh, or almost so, when standing naturally, e.g., German Short-haired Pointer breed standard. An almost impossible anatomical achievement in a normally angulated animal **(Figure 188a)**.
See **Figure 183**

Let down in hocks
See Well let down hocks

Set low hocks Mentioned in the Norwich Terrier breed standard.
See Well let down hocks

Sickle hocks A reference to the shape and contours of the hock joint components, i.e., lower thigh region above and rear pastern (metatarsus) below, when viewed from the side. In most breeds, when allowed to stand naturally, the rear pastern is positioned at an angle of approximately 90° to the ground, with a hock joint angle somewhere between 130° and 140°. Greater pastern slope tends to sharpen (i.e., lessen) the hock joint angle. Furthermore, it may cause an animal to 'stand under itself', and lowers the point of the hock, i.e., reduces the

Fig. 188a Well-bent or well-angulated hock

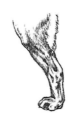
Fig. 188b Straight hock

Fig. 188c Sickle hock

distance between hock and ground. Sickle hocks are spoken of when the positions of lower thigh and rear pastern, viewed in profile, take on a sickle-shaped appearance **(Figure 188c)**. Conversely, dogs with hock angles more obtuse than normal, i.e., in excess of approximately 140°, are referred to as being 'straight in hock' or 'straight hocked' **(Figure 188b)**.
See **Figure 15**

Snatch or **Thrust of hocks** A reference to strong, purposeful flexion of the hock region. Assumed to be synonymous with powerful hindquarters drive, and mentioned in the Wire Fox Terrier breed standard.

Straight hocks A greater than desirable angle between the regions of the lower thigh and rear pastern.
See Sickle hocks

Weak hocks Broad, non-specific terminology, occasionally used to describe hock joints which vary from the norm, i.e., are insufficiently well-angulated for a specific breed, or over-angulated, turned in or turned out due to loose ligamentation, or in any way deformed.

Well-angulated hocks
See Well bent hocks

Well bent hocks syn. well-angulated hocks. Hock joints exhibiting the correct amount of rear angulation for a given breed. The opposite to a socalled 'straight' hock.
See Angulation, **Figure 15**

Well let down hocks syn. hocks close to the ground. Rear pasterns constructed and angulated in such a manner that the distance from point of hock to ground is correct for the breed concerned. Obviously, the shorter the metatarsus (rear pastern) and the more acute the hock joint angle, the more 'let down' do hocks appear.

HOLDERS Unusual terminology for the canine teeth, employed by the Rhodesian Ridgeback breed standard.

Hollow back
See Back Types

Hollow-breasted or **chested**
See Pigeon-breasted

Horizontal back
See Back Types

Horseshoe front
See Front Types

Hound ears
See Ear Types

HUCKLE The hip bones, or, more precisely, those portions of the pelvic wings that rise above the backline.

HUMERUS syn. arm.
See Forequarters

HUMP or **HUMPED BACK**
See Back Types

HUNTER, STAND LIKE A CLEVERLY MADE HUNTER An often-quoted phrase from the German Short-haired Pointer and Smooth Fox Terrier breed standards which succinctly and accurately describes the ideal anatomical construction and proportions of an animal required to possess a relatively short body coupled with maximum length of stride **(Figure 189)**.

Fig. 189 Stand like a cleverly made hunter: Fox Terrier (Smooth)

HYDROCEPHALUS syn. water on the brain. A congenital abnormality, not unusual in brachycephalic breeds, due to the increased collection of cerebral fluid in the brain case. Typified by marked enlargement as well as rounding of the cranium.

ILIUM One of the three bony components of the pelvic girdle, this is the bone surrounding the acetabulum or hip socket.
See Hindquarters.

INBREEDING A type of breeding programme employed to obtain improvements and/or 'fix' desirable physical characteristics or mental attributes through the mating of closely related animals, e.g., brother and sister, sire and daughter or mother and son. It is the opposite to outcrossing, which refers to breeding from totally unrelated animals within a given breed.

Line breeding may be referred to as the happy medium between inbreeding on the one hand and outcrossing on the other. By strict definition, it is an acceptable breeding programme based upon the mating of somewhat distantly related animals, i.e., cousins, uncles, aunts, nieces and nephews, rather than brothers, sisters, etc.

INCISIVE BONES
See Jaw

INCISORS
See Dentition, Jaws

INNER THIGH
See Thigh

INTERVERTEBRAL DISCS Soft cartilagenous structures located between individual spinal vertebrae to allow smooth frictionless movement of the spine **(Figure 190)**.
See Spinal column

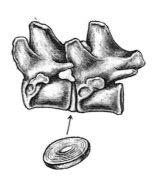

Fig. 190 Intervertebral disc

IRIS The coloured membrane surrounding the pupil.
See Eye anatomy, Eye colour

IRREGULAR BITE
See Bite

ISABELLA A straw-like fawn colour found in some breeds, e.g., Cane da Pastore Bergamasco and Dobermann.

ISCHIUM A component of the pelvic girdle.
See Hindquarters.

J

JABOT The name given to the apron of a Schipperke, especially that part situated between the front legs **(Figure 191)**.
See Apron

Fig. 191 Ruff or jabot: Schipperke

JACKET
See Coat

Jacket, tight fitting Taut skin and coat, fitting without any sign of looseness or wrinkles.

JASPER An opaque, usually red, brown or yellow variety of quartz. Used as an alternative description of the colour patches on a Pyrenean Mountain Dog.
See Badger

JAW; JAWS Those portions of the skull in which the teeth are located; two in number, i.e., the upper and lower jaws. The upper jaw consists of two identical halves, joined at the centre, and firmly and immovably attached to the rest of the skull, one on each side. Each half is made up of a maxilla on the side and an incisive bone at the front. Each incisive bone carries three incisors, and each maxilla one canine tooth, four premolars and two molars, i.e., a total of twenty teeth for the full upper jaw.

The lower jaw (syn. underjaw, mandible) also consists of right and left halves, firmly united at the centre front or mandibular symphysis, each half containing three lower incisors, one canine tooth, four premolars and three molars, i.e., a total of twenty-two for the complete lower set. Each mandible consists of a body (the tooth-bearing section) and a vertical portion or ramus at the back. The condyloid process at the top of each ramus articulates with the temporal bone at the side of the skull to form the temporo-mandibular joint. These joints are the only movable parts in the whole bony framework of the skull. The sections of the mandible bearing the incisor teeth, plus surrounding structures, form the chin area. Occasionally, and especially in some brachycephalic breeds, the mandibular symphysis tends to be rather loose. In such cases the mandibles are capable of more or less independent movement: a most serious defect, irrespective of breed.

The size and shape of the maxilla bones, and to a degree those of the incisive bones, have great bearing on the length, depth and general appearance of a dog's foreface. The relationship of fixed upper jaw to mobile lower jaw constitutes what is known as the 'bite'.
See Bite, Dentition, Skull, **Figure 75**

Level jaws Upper and lower jaws of equal length, but not necessarily a level or pincer bite.
See Bite, Mouth

Overshot jaw
See Bite

Punishing jaws; jaws of punishing strength Unusual terminology in some breed standards, e.g., Afghan Hound, Fox Terrier, for jaws sufficiently well-developed in all dimensions to enable an animal, in theory at least, to bring down and kill its prey, i.e., perform those duties for which it was originally intended.

Receding lower jaw syn. receding chin. A reference to a lower jaw underline that tapers rather

Fig. 192 Receding chin or lower jaw line: tapering jaws

severely, i.e., one that angles sharply backwards to a greater degree than normal, resulting in a muzzle relatively pointed in profile, but not necessarily associated with an overshot jaw **(Figure 192)**. Though an acutely tapering muzzle is accepted as normal in most of the Greyhound breeds, e.g., Borzoi, Collie, etc., a receding lower jaw line is considered a fault in most other breeds.

Tapering jaws One in which the lines of the upper and lower jaws taper gradually towards the end of the muzzle in varying degrees.
See Muzzle, tapering and **Figure 225**

Tight-lipped jaws The visual outline created by relatively thin lips, closely following the bony jaw outline; the opposite to fleshy or pendulous lip appearance, e.g., Brittany Spaniel.
See **Figure 201**

Undershot jaw
See Bite

JEWELLED EYE
See Eye Colour

JOWLS Heavy, fleshy or pendulous lips, such as in the British Bulldog.
See **Figures 57, 204** and **290**

K

KEEL The rounded curve or outline of the lower chest (brisket) of a Dachshund between the prosternum and end of breastbone, resembling the keel of a boat; also referred to in the Blood-hound breed standard **(Figure 193)**.

Fig. 193 Keel: Dachshund

Clipped keel Used by Dachshund fanciers to describe an abnormally short sternum, usually one that blends rather abruptly into the lower line of the abdomen **(Figure 194)**.

Fig. 194 Clipped keel

KINK TAIL
See Tail Types

KISSING SPOT The name occasionally given to the lozenge mark on the head of the Blenheim variety of the Cavalier King Charles Spaniel.
See **Figures 34** and **212**

KISS·MARKS Tan spots on the cheeks of black-and-tan coloured dogs, such as the Dobermann and Rottweiler; also black-and-tan-and-white dogs, such as the Bernese Mountain Dog **(Figure 195)**.

Fig. 195 Kiss marks: Dobermann

KNEE; KNEE JOINT Borrowed from human anatomy and used as a synonym for the stifle joint in the rear leg. Sometimes also used incorrectly in reference to the wrist or carpus region, e.g., 'knees large and strong' (Sussex Spaniel) or 'there may be wrinkles of skin between knee and foot' (Basset Hound).
See Stifle, Hindquarters

KNEECAP syn. patella. A relatively small bone, located in a groove at the lower end of the thigh bone.
See Patellar dislocation, Hindquarters, **Figure 181**

KNIT; KNITTING
See Plait

KNUCKLING; KNUCKLING OVER A forward bending of the leg at the wrist joint when standing. A not uncommon habit, due to faulty construction, in some short-legged dogs, e.g., Basset Hound (where the breed standard lists it as a fault), also in long-legged Hound breeds with upright shoulder blade placement and/or short, steep pasterns, e.g., Harriers, in which a slight knuckling over is not considered faulty **(Figure 196)**.

Fig. 196 Knuckling over in Basset Hound (left) and Foxhound (right)

L

LACHRYMAL GLANDS The tear-producing glands, situated at the inner corners of the eyes, one on each side.
See Eye Anatomy, **Figure 109**

LANK An adjective used as in 'long, low and lank' (A.K.C.'s Skye Terrier breed standard) to mean lean.

LATERAL Anatomical terminology for 'pertaining to the side', e.g., in the British Bulldog breed standard 'the chest should be laterally round', i.e., the ribs well rounded outwards.

LAYBACK Describes the position, in profile, of the nose in some brachycephalic breeds (e.g., British Bulldog, Pekingese), i.e., a nose that lies within a straight line drawn from point of chin to forehead is said to be well 'laid back' **(Figure 197)**.
See **Figure 253**

Fig. **197** Lay-back: British Bulldog

LAY OF SHOULDERS
See Forequarters, Angulation

LEATHER The cartilagenous lobe of the outer ear. A term most commonly used in reference to Gundog breeds.
See Ear Anatomy

LEATHER ENDS Short-coated or partially hairless ear tips on otherwise well-coated ears, e.g., Brittany and Clumber Spaniels.
See **Figure 49b**

LEGGY syn. high on leg. Tall, but not necessarily rangy, high-off-the-ground appearance. Normally caused by two conditions or combination thereof, namely: (a) excessive length of leg for a

Fig. **198** Leggy, square appearance

particular breed, and (b) inadequate chest depth in relation to leg length. In some breeds legginess is required, e.g., in the Greyhound group **(Figure 198)**.

LEGS, BANDY A reference to the appearance imparted by outward bent forearms and/or hind legs curved out laterally from hip to hock, i.e., bowhocked. Also referred to as 'barrel' legs or barrel hocked, e.g., Great Dane breed standard (A.K.C.).
See **Figures 144, 152** and **272**

LEGS WELL UNDER BODY This phrase has different meanings. When the dog is viewed in profile, it refers to the position of front or hind legs which are set well underneath the body, resulting from correct angulation; it is mentioned in American and English breed standards, e.g., Afghan Hound, Whippet, Australian Silky Terrier, Curly-Coated Retriever, Pembroke Welsh Corgi, etc. **(Figure 199)**. When taken front on, it is a reference to a body placed well on top of the legs and not slung between them **(Figure 200)**.

LENGTH
See Body length

LEONINE Specifically applied to Chow Chow expression, meaning 'lionlike'.

LEVEL BACK
See Back Types

Fig. 199 Legs well under body (left) and legs forward placed (right)

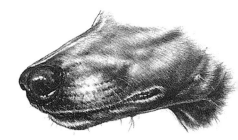

Fig. 201 Clean lips: Whippet

Fig. 200 Legs well under body (left) and body slung between legs (right)

LEVEL BITE
See Bite

LEVEL JAWS; LEVEL JAWED
See Jaws, Level jaws, Bite

LEVEL MOUTH
See Mouth

LINE BREEDING
See Inbreeding

LINTY COAT
See Coat Types

LIPS Technically, the fleshy portions of the upper and lower jaws covering the teeth, i.e., the surrounds of the mouth cavity. Definition for practical purposes is more difficult, as the lips tend to blend without clear lines of demarcation into the regions of muzzle, cheeks and chin. The upper lips commence in the area just below the nose and run downwards, covering the upper teeth, and end at the lip margins. To the side of the face, the upper lips merge into the cheeks. The lower lips begin at the lip margins and cover the lower teeth, finally blending with the chin area. The lip edges are frequently heavily pigmented. They are rather narrow and devoid of hair except on the front portions of the upper lips. The angle

of junction of upper and lower lips is termed the labial commisure **(Figure 201)**.

Whilst the above information is unquestionably correct in anatomical terms, the wording of some breed standards, e.g., Gordon Setter, would indicate that the word lip is applied to the margin only, the rest being referred to as the flews.

LIP TYPES

Fluttering lips Unusual terminology for excessively pendulous and often rather thin or papery lips overhanging the lower jaw, thereby creating the illusion of a deep, square muzzle; used to describe a fault in the A.K.C.'s Great Dane breed standard.

Hare lips A congenital abnormality, due to arrested facial development, resulting in irregular fissure formation at the junction of the two upper lip halves, i.e., at the naso-labial line or philtrum **(Figure 202)**. While hare lips can and do occur in most breeds, the condition is more common in brachycephalic types, e.g., Boxer, Pekingese.

Fig. 202 Hare lip

Hound-like lips Well-developed, deep, pendulous flews tending to be squared off in front. Typical of Bloodhound, Beagle, Basset Hound, etc., but considered as undesirable in some breeds, e.g., Cavalier King Charles Spaniel **(Figure 203)**.

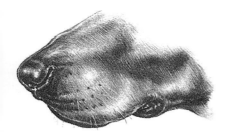

Fig. 203 Overhung top lip

Overhung lips syn. pendulous lips. An unusual description found in the German Short-haired Pointer standard, used to describe a fault.
See Lippy

Pendulous lips Full, loosely-hanging lips, i.e., flews, hiding the jaw line when viewed in profile. Typified by the Clumber Spaniel (lower lip), Bloodhound (upper lip), but listed as a fault in other breeds, e.g., Hungarian Vizsla **(Figures 204 and 205)**.

Fig. 204 Pendulous lower lips: extreme: St. Bernard

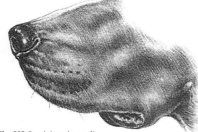

Fig. 205 Pendulous lower lips

Receding lips syn. receding jaw, receding chin. A reference to a muzzle which is relatively pointed in profile, e.g., Borzoi, in contrast to one ending bluntly.

Split upper lips Incomplete union of the upper lip halves at their lower borders; the early stage of hare lip development.

Tight lips
See Jaws, Tight-lipped

LIPPY Pendulous lips, developed to the point of excessiveness; also referred to as overhung lips **(Figure 206)**.

Fig. 206 Lippy: St. Bernard

LOADED SHOULDERS
See Shoulders

LOBE The cartilage of the external ear.
See Ear Anatomy

LOBE-SHAPED or **LOBULAR EARS**
See Ear Types

LOIN; LOINS The lumbar area, extending from the end of the rib cage to the start of the pelvis, i.e., the upper section of the couplings region.

LOIN TYPES

Arched loins A request of many breed standards, especially in the Hound group, e.g., Dachshund; symptomatic of strength and agility in that area, but only if due to muscular, not structural, development over the spine **(Figure 207)**.

Fig. 207 Arched loins

Light in loins A request for limited, not excessive, loin development, thereby creating the desirable waist or 'waisted appearance' of, for example, the Staffordshire Bull Terrier, Miniature Pinscher and Basenji **(Figure 208)**.

Fig. 208 Light in loin

Sagging loins An anatomical weakness due to a combination of loins both overlong and insufficiently well-muscled; this causes the backline over the coupling area to droop or sway **(Figure 209)**.

Fig. 209 Sagging loins

Slightly tucked loins Reference in the A.K.C.'s breed standard of the American Staffordshire Terrier to 'slightly drawn in loins', giving a waisted appearance as seen from above **(Figure 210)**.

Fig. 210 Loins slightly tucked: Staffordshire Terrier

LOLLING TONGUE
See Tongue, lolling

LONG BACK
See Back Types: Long back

LONG COUPLED; LONG IN COUPLING
See Coupling

LOOSE COUPLED; LOOSE IN COUPLING
See Coupling

LOOSE IN ELBOWS
See Elbows, out at

LOW SET; LOW SET BUILD A reference to the distance from the ground of the brisket and/or underline in general. A dog is said to be 'low set' when such distance is relatively short, especially as compared to height at the withers and/or distance from withers to brisket. Examples of normally low set breeds include Sealyham Terrier, Dachshund, Basset Hound, etc. 'Up on leg' or 'of high station' are used to describe the opposite type of conformation **(Figure 211)**.

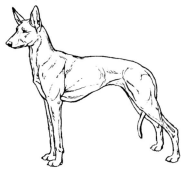

Fig. 211 Of high station: up on leg (top) and of low station: low set

LOW SET TAIL
See Tail, low set

LOW STATION; LOW IN STATION
See Station

LOWER ARM The region encompassing the radius and ulna bones.
See Forequarters

LOWER JAW syn. mandible.
See Jaw

LOWER THIGH The area surrounding the tibia and fibula bones.
See Hindquarters

LOZENGE MARK The chestnut-coloured spot or thumb print situated on the skull between the ears, as seen in the Blenheim varieties of the Cavalier King Charles and King Charles Spaniels. For preference centrally placed, the lozenge mark or beauty spot (sometimes known as the 'kissing spot') is a highly prized characteristic of these breeds **(Figure 212)**.
See Beauty spot, Spot and **Figure 34**

Fig. 212 Lozenge spot, lobular ear: Cavalier King Charles Spaniel

LUMBAR Anatomical terminology appertaining to the loin region, e.g., lumbar vertebrae.

LUMBER Excessive muscular and/or bony development, to the point of being superfluous; also heavy, cloddy build, with cumbersome movement. The Flat Coated Retriever breed standard, under the heading of 'General Appearance', for example, employs the phrase 'showing power without lumber'. This is interpreted as 'strength without cloddiness'. Similarly, the Dalmatian breed standard states 'free from coarseness and lumber'.

LUMPY SHOULDERS
See Shoulders

LUNG ROOM, PLENTY OF Inferring chest dimensions sufficient to permit optimum lung and heart development. A prerequisite for stamina and exercise tolerance.
See Chest capacity

LUXATION Synonym of dislocation, as applied to joints, e.g., patellar luxation.

M

MAKING THE WHEEL
See Tail Types

MALAR BONE
See Zygomatic arch

MANDIBLE syn. lower jaw, underjaw.
See Jaw

MANE syn. shawl. Longish, usually fairly coarse hair arising from the ridge of the neck, then falling over to one side, e.g., Chinese Crested Dog **(Figure 213)**.
See Ruff, **Figure 218**

Fig. 213 Mane: Pekingese

MANTLE Darkly pigmented or heavily shaded area on the coat, similar in distribution to a blanket but more extensive, involving the neck, shoulders, back and sides. Most frequently used in European short-coated hound breed standards, e.g., Levesque, Finnish Hound, Artois, Polish Hound, Poitevin, also Alaskan Malamute, etc.
See **Figure 41**

MARBLED EYES
See Eye Colour

MARKINGS Generally used in reference to white areas distributed on a coloured background. Many such markings occur in dogs. Identification and nomenclature are related to horse terminology, e.g., star, blaze, stocking, etc. The more common types are discussed under separate headings.

MASK Dark shading of varying degrees about the head, forming a mask-like pattern. In the Boxer and Great Dane, for example, the mask involves the muzzle region **(Figure 214)**. In the Alaskan

Fig. 214 Mask: Great Dane

Fig. 215 Cap and mask: Alaskan Malamute

Malamute the mask is situated over the top part of the head and around the eyes **(Figure 215)**.

The word 'mask' is used also in describing short-coated areas about the head of an otherwise long-coated breed, e.g., German Shepherd Dog, Shetland Sheepdog.
See **Figure 104b**

MASTER HAIR Another name for guard hair, used, for example, in the Eskimo Dog breed standard.
See Guard hairs

MAXILLA; MAXILLAE
See Jaws

MEASUREMENTS Accurate measurements of height, length, chest depth, etc., are of vital importance in the breeding and judging of dogs. **Figure 216** shows the points from which such measurements should be taken, unless stated otherwise in respective breed standards. *See* Height and Body Length

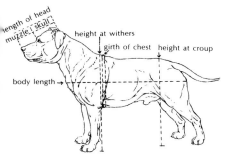

Fig. 216 Measurements

MEDIAN LINE syn. flute, furrow. Longitudinal groove, formed by bone formation and/or muscular development, running along from the centre of the skull, i.e., the frontal bone junction, towards the stop. A requirement of some breeds, e.g., Weimaraner, Hungarian Vizsla. In America, Springer Spaniel fanciers refer to the median line as 'the groove or fluting between the eyes' **(Figure 217)**.

Fig. 217 Median line, central furrow or groove: Weimaraner

MELON PIPS
See Pips

MERLE; MERLING Coat colour, due to a dominant colour pattern factor, distinguished by the presence of irregular, dark blotches against a lighter background of the same general basic pigment. 'Merle' is normally applied to long-coated breeds, an exception being the Smooth-coated

Collie; 'dapple' is used for short-coated varieties, e.g., Dachshund. The most common type of merle is 'blue merle' (i.e., black patches or streaks on a blue-grey background), e.g., Collie, Cardigan Welsh Corgi. Other kinds include liver merle, red merle, etc. **(Figure 218)**. *See* **Figure 73**

Fig. 218 Merle colour pattern on short- and long-coated breed

MESATICEPHALIC
See Skull Types

METACARPAL PAD syn. communal pad.
See Feet anatomy

METACARPUS The pastern region.
See Forequarters

METATARSUS syn. rear pastern.
See Hindquarters

MILK TEETH
See Dentition

MINCING ACTION or **GAIT**
See Action

MISMARK; MISMARKED A dog coloured or marked in any way contrary to the requirements of the breed standard, e.g., white areas on the body of the Pembroke Welsh Corgi.

MODELLING
See Chiselling

MOLARS
See Dentition, Jaws

MOLE Raised marks or spots on the cheeks of some breeds, e.g., Pug, in most instances with a few tufts of hair erupting from their centre **(Figure 219)**.

Fig. 219 Mole: Whippet

MOLERO A space, hole or gap in the centre of the skull, due to incomplete union of the frontal bones, covered only by skin and hair. A specialised feature of some Chihuahuas. The incomplete protection so effected renders such a dog liable to serious injury **(Figure 220)**.

Fig. 220 Position of molero: Chihuahua

MONGREL A dog of mixed breed, i.e., incorporating more than two varieties, and not deliberately planned. A crossbred dog, on the other hand, is the result of crossing two recognised breeds, either by accident or design, to establish a new variety or improve an existing one.

MONORCHID; MONORCHIDISM
See Cryptorchidism

MOTTLE; MOTTLED Basically a bi-coloured pattern consisting of dark, roundish blotches superimposed upon a lightish background, giving an overall uniform appearance, e.g., the blue-mottled variety of the Australian Cattle Dog.
See **Figure 298**

MOUSTACHE Longish hair, of varying texture, arising from the lips and sides of the face to create a moustache-like effect. Typified by the

Scottish Deerhound ('a good silky moustache'), Wire-haired Pointing Griffon ('hard, wiry moustache'), etc. **(Figure 221)**.
See **Figures 33, 140** and **353**

Fig. 221 Moustache and beard: Scottish Deerhound

MOUTH
See Bite and Jaws

Corners of the mouth syn. labial commisure.
See Lips

MOUTH TYPES

Crooked mouth Usually a reference to a wry mouth, but technically any variation from a normal bite.
See Bite

Level mouth Probably one of the most confused and strongly debated requirements of breed standards. By strict definition, the request for a level mouth simply refers to upper and lower jaws of equal length, in which the opposing dental arches (i.e., the two rows of incisor teeth, upper and lower) are lined up horizontally to meet edge to edge when the mouth is closed, appearing as a perfectly matched pair. Provided the angle of eruption of the incisor teeth is correct, i.e., as square as possible to the jaw, a level mouth is a prerequisite to the often-requested scissors bite **(Figure 222)**. Some breed standards, especially American ones, use the phrase 'teeth level' in place of 'mouth level', while others refer to 'teeth level with scissors bite'; all this is con-

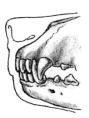

Fig. 222 Level mouth or jaws

fusing terminology. 'Mouth level and scissors bite' (Sussex Spaniel) is self-explanatory, meaning jaws of even length with scissors bite. 'Teeth level' is not. It could be taken as synonymous with 'mouth level'; on the other hand, it might well refer to incisors the contact tables of which are correctly aligned horizontally.
See Bite, Jaws

Parrot mouth An overshot bite.
See Bite

Roof of mouth
See Palate

Scrambled mouth A term used mainly by Lhasa Apso fanciers, meaning misplaced and jumbled incisors.

Shark mouth A synonym of overshot, i.e., a receding lower jaw.
See Bite

Soft mouth A reference to hunting dogs capable of performing their duties, i.e., retrieving game, without causing physical damage to their prey. A 'soft mouth' is a desirable quality due to influence of temperament, rather than physical attributes.

Wry mouth A type of mouth in which the lower jaw is twisted to one side, placing the upper and lower jaws out of line with one another. A relatively common fault in brachycephalic (short-faced) breeds, e.g., British Bulldog, Pekingese **(Figure 223)**.
See Jaws, Bite

Fig. 223 Wry mouth

MOVEMENT
See Action, Gait

MOVING CLOSE
See Gait

MULTUM IN PARVO Latin for 'much encompassed in little'. Used in the Pug breed standard to denote compactness coupled with strength, within the confines of a relatively small frame.
See **Figure 62**

MUSCLE BOUND Excessive development of individual muscle groups, usually on and around the

limbs, resulting in relatively restricted, cumbersome and lumbering movement.

MUSCULATION The disposition, development and arrangement of muscles; especially as applied to specific and/or localised muscle groups, e.g., in the Weimaraner breed standard, 'hindquarter musculation well-developed'.

MUSIC Specialist terminology for the baying sounds made by hounds at work.

MUZZLE That portion of the skull in front of the brain case, comprising the forward portions of both upper and lower jaws. In dolichocephalic (long-headed) breeds, the muzzle is long, sometimes greater than half the total length of skull. The reverse position holds true for brachycephalic (short-faced) breeds. Apart from length, other muzzle dimensions are width, depth and diameter as shown in **Figure 216**.
See Face, **Figures 120 to 123**

MUZZLE TYPES

Blunt or **square muzzle** syn. truncated muzzle. The opposite to a pointed muzzle. As explained in the Mastiff breed standard: 'Blunt and cut off square, thus forming a right angle with the upper line of the face' **(Figure 224)**.

Fig. 224 Blunt muzzle: Pointer

Pinched or **snipy muzzle** Over-refined (the emphasis being on the word 'over'), weak construction of the foreface, especially as viewed from above; normally employed to describe a fault. Muzzles so affected usually appear too chiselled about their junction with the skull, as well as too pointed at the tips. Whilst highly refined muzzles are acceptable in some breeds, e.g., Norwegian Puffin Dog, numerous breed standards such as Collie (Rough), list such construction as faulty. The importance, when judging, of differentiating between a fine muzzle such as, for example, requested in the Pomeranian breed standard, and a pinched muzzle, cannot be over-emphasised.
See **Figure 56**

Pointed muzzle
See Tapering muzzle, **Figure 225**

Root of muzzle Unusual terminology employed in the Boxer breed standard for the area of junction between the stop and foreface, i.e., the opposite end to the tip of the nose.

Short muzzle syn. stubby muzzle. A feature of

Fig. 225 Pointed muzzle: fine muzzle tapering: Whippet

brachycephalic breeds, e.g., Pug, Boston Terrier. A muzzle that is shorter than half the total length of skull **(Figure 226)**.

Fig. 226 Short, blunt muzzle: French Bulldog

Snipy muzzle
See Pinched muzzle

Square muzzle
See Blunt muzzle

Stubby muzzle
See Short muzzle

Tapering muzzle syn. wedge-shaped muzzle, pointed muzzle. A muzzle of greater diameter at its origin (i.e., at base of stop) than at its apex. Such taper may vary from mild **(Figure 227)**, e.g., Pharaoh Hound, to severe, e.g., Greyhound breeds **(Figure 228)**. Acutely tapering muzzles are referred to as 'pointed' **(Figure 225)**, in contrast to those ending in a blunt or squared-off fashion **(Figure 177)**.

Fig. 227 Wedge-shaped muzzle: Pharaoh Hound

Fig. 228 Tapering or long wedge muzzle: Borzoi

Fig. 229 Muzzle band: Boston Terrier

Wedge-shaped muzzle (Figure 228).
See Muzzle, tapering

MUZZLE BAND Used specifically in the Boston Terrier breed standard to describe this breed's white markings around the muzzle **(Figure 229)**.

N

NAPE The area of the junction of the skull base to the top of the neck.
See **Figure 11**

NARROW FRONT
See Front Types

NASAL BONE The bony section of the foreface forming the top edge of the muzzle.
See Skull anatomy, **Figure 291**

NASAL SEPTUM The bony partition dividing right and left nasal cavities.

NASO-LABIAL LINE syn. philtrum. The groove at the junction of the left and right upper lip halves. Mentioned in the Boxer breed standard, this furrow begins at the tip of the nose, runs vertically down and ends at the bottom edge of the upper lip.
See Lips, Nose anatomy, and **Figure 239**

NECK That section of the body between the head and shoulder region, beginning at the nape and ending at the neck/shoulder junction or 'blendin'. The neck has a topline and underline; the former, if curved or arched, is referred to as a crest **(Figure 230)**.

Fig. 231 Stuffy, short, bull or thick neck

appearance in profile, due to exaggerated thickness and coarse neck/shoulder junction **(Figure 231)**.

Clean neck syn. dry neck. A neck region with tight-fitting skin, devoid of excessive amounts of loose skin, wrinkles or dewlap; the opposite to a throaty or wet neck **(Figure 232)**.

Fig. 232 Clean, dry neck: Greyhound

Crested neck syn. well-arched neck. A reference to well-developed neck muscles, particularly those responsible for the arch or crest on top **(Figure 233)**.
See Crest

Dry neck syn. clean neck.

Ewe neck syn. concave neck, upside-down neck. A neck in which the topline is concave rather than convex. A decided anatomical weakness, with a base circumference usually not much, if any, greater than that at the head and neck junction **(Figure 234)**.

Fig. 230 Normal well-set neck

NECK TYPES

Arched neck
See Crested neck

Bull neck A powerfully muscled, strong neck; very masculine and usually characterised by an accentuated crest. Often of rather short, stuffy

Fig. 233 Well arched or crested neck

Fig. 236 Long, reachy neck

Fig. 234 Ewe neck

Goose neck syn. swan neck. An elongated, tubular-shaped neck, lacking strength and cresting, with a neck base of similar circumference to that at the head/neck junction **(Figure 235)**.

Fig. 235 Swan or goose neck

Reachy neck A neck of adequate length, well-muscled, yet refined and elegant. The opposite to a short or stuffy neck **(Figure 236)**.

Round neck A neck, the trunk of which is round in transverse section, e.g., American Water Spaniel, in contrast to the more usual elliptical shape.

Stuffy neck A short, blocky and inelegant neck, often too heavily covered in muscles **(Figure 231)**.
See Bull neck

Fig. 237 Wet neck: Dogue de Bordeaux

Swan neck syn. goose neck. Listed as a fault in the A.K.C.'s Dachshund breed standard **(Figure 235)**.

Throaty neck syn. wet neck. One in which the skin is loose and showing wrinkles, especially dewlap. The opposite to a dry neck **(Figure 237)**.
See Throatiness

Upside-down neck
See Ewe neck

Well-set neck A reference to a neck placed correctly into the shoulder region with an almost imperceptible blend-in.

Wet neck
See Throaty neck

NECK RUFF
See Ruff

NECK, UPRIGHT CARRIAGE OF Lofty carriage, reducing the angle between neck and horizontal line of thoracic spine; the head is held high, creating an appearance of nobility **(Figure 238)**.

Fig. 238 Upright neck

NERVE, OLFACTORY
See Olfactory nerve

NICTITATING MEMBRANE
See Third eyelid

NIGHT BLINDNESS
See Progressive retinal atrophy

NON-UNITING ANCONEAL PROCESS
See Un-united anconeal process

NOSE Technically, the term nose refers to the external nose, its associated nasal cartilages and nasal cavity **(Figure 239)**. To most dog fanciers, however, the word nose simply means the external portions, or even the muzzle as a whole, e.g., long nose, short nose, etc. Evidence of this lies in the use of descriptions like butterfly nose, dudley nose, etc. The external nose consists of a movable cartilagenous framework, attached by ligaments to the surrounding bony case. Its skin covering is relatively short-haired, irrespective of breed. The front portion is hairless and features individually characteristic nasal patterns **(Figure 240)**. Viewed front on, there are two nostrils joined at the centre by the philtrum or naso-labial line.

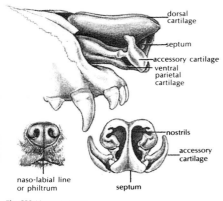

Fig. 239 Nose structure

dorsal cartilage
septum
accessory cartilage
ventral parietal cartilage
nostrils
accessory cartilage
naso-labial line or philtrum
septum

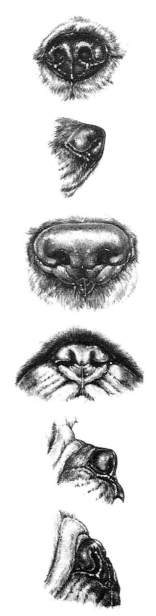

Fig. 240 Variations in nose types and shapes

NOSE TYPES

Aquiline nose
See Ram's nose, Foreface

Brown or **liver nose** An acceptable colour in some breeds, e.g., German Short-haired Pointer (brown), Irish Water Spaniel and Sussex Spaniel (liver) **(Figure 241)**.
See Self-coloured nose

Fig. 241 Brown, liver or self-coloured nose

Butterfly nose syn. spotted nose. A partially unpigmented nose of irregular flecked appearance. Typical of harlequin-patterned or merle-coloured dogs, e.g., Great Dane, Cardigan Welsh Corgi, but listed as undesirable in numerous breed standards. The time of completion of full nasal pigmentation tends to vary from breed to breed and even strains within a given breed. When judging, it is important, therefore, not to penalise too severely for incomplete pigmentation at too early an age **(Figure 242)**.
See Flesh Marks

Fig. 242 Butterfly nose: Great Dane

Cherry nose
See Dudley nose

Dudley nose The name given to a weakly pigmented, flesh-coloured nose. Other names applied to the dudley nose syndrome include 'cherry nose', 'putty nose' and 'flesh nose' **(Figure 243)**.

Flesh or **Flesh-coloured nose** An evenly-coloured nose, similar in all respects to the so-called 'dudley' nose; the difference being that the term

Fig. 243 Dudley nose

'dudley' is used to describe a fault, whilst 'flesh-coloured' is used in breed standards where such pigmentation is acceptable, e.g., Weimaraner, Clumber Spaniel, Welsh Springer Spaniel, Spinone Italiano, Pharaoh Hound **(Figure 244)**.

Fig. 244 Pink, cherry or flesh-coloured nose

Liver-coloured nose
See Brown nose

Partly unpigmented nose Self-explanatory, such colouring need not necessarily be of a permanent nature, nor is it always to be regarded as a fault, as climatic, environmental and nutritional factors may cause temporary loss of nasal pigment **(Figure 245)**.
See Butterfly nose

Fig. 245 Partly unpigmented nose

Pink nose A lightly pigmented nose, in contrast to a black or brown one. In most instances a pink nose is considered a fault. There are some exceptions however, e.g., St. Germain Pointer **(Figure 244)**.

Putty nose
See Dudley nose

Ram's nose syn. aquiline nose. A facial profile in which the topline of the foreface is relatively straight except for the nasal cartilage which dips downwards: this is in direct contrast to a Roman nose that curves in convex fashion in an unbroken line from stop to tip of nose, e.g., Bull Terrier. In the Scottish Deerhound breed standard, the term aquiline nose is used in place of ram's nose **(Figure 246a)**.
See **Figures 107** and **228**

Fig. 246a Ram's nose

Fig. 246b Roman nose

Roman nose (Figures 123a and 246b).
See Ram's nose

Self-coloured nose A nose of similar, preferably identical, pigmentation to a dog's body colour,

e.g., a chocolate-coloured nose on a chocolate-and-tan Miniature Pinscher **(Figure 241)**.

Smudge nose
See Snow nose

Snow nose syn. smudge nose. Specialist terminology in the Siberian Husky breed standard for a nose that is normally solid black, but acquires a pink streak in winter: an acceptable characteristic in that breed. The snow nose syndrome is frequently seen in other breeds also, e.g., Labrador Retriever **(Figure 247)**.

Fig. 247 Snow or smudge nose

Spotted nose
See Butterfly nose

NOSTRILS The two external orifices (openings) of the nose. Many variations exist in shape, size, etc.
See Nose

Flared nostrils Wide open nostrils, designed for maximum air intake, with slightly rounded cartilagenous ends, e.g., Bouvier des Flandres **(Figure 248)**.

Fig. 248 Flared nostrils

O

OBLIQUELY-PLACED EYES
See Eye Types

OBLONG EYES
See Eye Types

OCCIPUT syn. occipital bone, peak, apex. An important anatomical feature and landmark when judging dogs. References to the occiput, in one form or another, occur in most breed standards, e.g., 'pronounced occipital bone' (Pointer), 'prominent occiput' (Afghan Hound), 'occipital bone inconspicuous, rounded rather than peaked or angular' (English Springer Spaniel, A.K.C.). The occipital crest is the ridge formed by the occipital bone at the back of the skull where it joins with the parietal bones on either side. Its function is to serve as an area for muscle attachment. The highest and rearmost part of the occipital crest is known as the occiput **(Figure 249)**.

Fig. 249 Occiput or peak: Bleu de Gascoigne

OCCIPITAL CREST
See Occiput

OESTRUS syn. season, heat. That portion of the reproductive cycle during which a bitch exhibits sexual interest in male partners. Preceded by a period of pro-oestrus, oestrus in the bitch usually lasts for approximately twenty-one days, followed by metoestrus. The external signs of oestrus include (a) swelling of the vulval lips, (b) the appearance, sometimes profuse, of blood-stained discharge, (c) unusual behaviour pattern, e.g., seeking out the company of dogs.

OLFACTORY NERVE One of the twelve cranial nerves of the dog, this is mentioned in the Field Spaniel breed standard in relation to this breed's comparatively long muzzle, the suggestion being that muzzle development, especially in length, plays an important part in determining the scenting ability of a given breed. The scientific basis of this theory is open to question, as, in fact, the branches of the olfactory nerve, responsible for picking up scent and directing it to the brain proper, are located around the area of the skull and foreface junction and do not penetrate to any great degree into the muzzle as such. Hence muzzle length per se would seemingly have little bearing on scenting ability **(Figure 250)**.

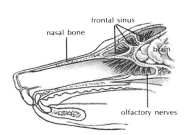

Fig. 250 Olfactory nerves

OLECRANON PROCESS syn. point of elbow.
See Forequarters

OPEN COAT
See Coat Types

ORANGE BELTON An English Setter colour.
See Belton

ORB syn. eyeball.

ORBIT The cavity in which the eyeball is located, i.e., the eye socket, e.g., in the Bloodhound breed standard, 'eyes deeply sunk in the orbits'.

ORBITAL MUSCLES, PROMINENT A greater degree than usual of muscular development above the eyes, creating an illusion of heavy brows, e.g., Alaskan Malamute **(Figure 251)**.

ORNAMENTATION An alternative to 'furnish-

Fig. 251 Prominent orbital muscles: Alaskan Malamute

ings', used in A.K.C.'s breed standard of the Belgian Sheepdog.
See Furnishings

OTTER TAIL
See Tail Types

OUT AT ELBOWS, OUT IN ELBOWS
See Elbows

OUTCROSSING
See Inbreeding

OVAL EYES
See Eye Types

OVAL FEET
See Feet Types

OVERBUILT
See Back Types

OVERFILL The opposite to 'chiselling'. Mentioned as a fault in the A.K.C.'s Shetland Sheepdog breed standard, overfill refers to a greater amount of bone and/or muscle than desired below, between and above the eyes, creating a bumpy or coarse appearance in that area **(Figure 252)**.

Fig. 252 Overfill

OVERHANG Well-developed, forward arched, extended and pronounced forehead/brow, which, when viewed in profile, overhangs the nose, e.g., Pekingese **(Figure 253)**.

OVERHUNG LIPS
See Lips

Fig. 253 Overhang: Pekingese

OVERLAY A mantle or blanket of dark shaded colour superimposed on a lighter background, e.g., 'black overlay' (Belgian Malinois). Synonymous with 'sable'.
See **Figure 279**

OVER-REACH
See Gait

OVERSHOT
See Bite

P

PACE
See Gait

PACK In a Poodle, prepared in the English lion clip, that portion of the coat situated over the loin/rump area. Ideally said to be astrakhan both in appearance and texture **(Figure 254)**.

Fig. 254 Pack: Poodle

PAD, PADS
See Feet Anatomy

PADS, SPRINGY; PADS, WELL-CUSHIONED
Thick toe pads, furnished with adequate amounts of elastic tissue to provide an appropriate cushioning effect during movement. The opposite to thin, hard toe pads.
See **Figure 125**

PADDING A specialist term used in reference to lip thickness of some breeds, e.g., Boxer, British Bulldog. In the Boxer, for example, to obtain correct appearance and expression, the lips must be 'well-padded' or 'have sufficient padding' **(Figure 255)**.
See **Figures 72** and **120**

PADDLING
See Gait

PALATE The partly bony, partly fleshy partition separating the respiratory and digestive passages of the head. In anatomical terms, the palate is divided into (a) the hard palate in front; of bony composition, commencing immediately behind the upper incisor teeth, and forming the major

Fig. 255 Padding

portion of the roof of the mouth, and (b) the soft palate, of fleshy consistency, and virtually a continuation backwards of the hard palate.
See **Figure 166**

Cleft palate A congenital defect, especially common in brachycephalic (short-faced) breeds, in which the two bony halves of the hard palate fail to unite completely along the centre line, leaving a gap between them **(Figure 256)**.

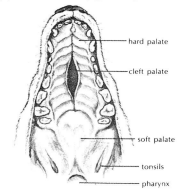

hard palate

cleft palate

soft palate

tonsils

pharynx

Fig. 256 Cleft palate

Soft palate Located at the roof of the mouth, the soft palate is a soft fleshy extension of the hard palate in front, continuing in a backwards direction to end near the larynx or Adam's apple. In the dog, the soft palate is especially well-developed. In some short-faced (brachycephalic) breeds it may, in fact, be so long as to interfere with the free passage of air into the windpipe. This condition, referred to as a 'prolonged soft palate', may endanger an animal's life, particularly in hot and/or humid climates. Excessive development of the soft palate, as described, is thought to be of inherited origin.
See **Figure 256**

PALPEBRAL FISSURE
See **Figure 349**, Eye Anatomy

PANCREATIC DEGENERATIVE ATROPHY A not uncommon disease of the canine pancreas (sweetbread), which, in affected animals, tends to undergo degenerative regression, resulting in the patient's inability to digest and/or absorb food, bringing about an undernourished and unthrifty appearance.

PANTS Used in the A.K.C.'s Chihuahua breed standard as a synonym for breeches, breeching or trousers.
See **Figure 46a**

PAPER FEET
See Feet Types

PARROT JAW, PARROT MOUTH
See Bite: Overshot bite

PARTI-COLOUR; PARTI-COLOURED Coat colour pattern broken up into two colours, one of which is white, in more or less equal proportions.

PASTERN The metacarpus, i.e., the region between the carpus (wrist) above, and the digits (foot) below. The pasterns of different breeds exhibit great variations in type, strength, length and slope, depending upon usage. To quote two opposing examples: in the Foxhound the pasterns called for are relatively short and upright; in the German Shepherd Dog, on the other hand, they are fairly long and sloping. The most common types are described below.
See Forequarters and **Figures 13** and **14**

Bare pasterns Afghan Hound specialists' terminology for pasterns devoid of long hair. An acceptable feature of this breed. In the A.K.C.'s version of the Afghan Hound breed standard, bare pasterns are referred to as 'cuffs' **(Figure 257a)**.

Broken-down pasterns
See Pasterns, down in

Distended pastern joint The rather unattractive knobbly appearance, especially when viewed

Fig. 257a Bare pasterns: Afghan Hound

front on, of an enlarged carpal or pastern joint. Common causes include coarse bone, injury, arthritis, etc.

Down in pasterns syn. sunken pasterns, falling pasterns. Pasterns with a greater than desirable slope away from the perpendicular, when viewed side on. Apart from being unsightly, excessively sloping or broken-down pasterns tend to reduce exercise tolerance, as dogs so affected tire more readily than sound animals. Causes include greater than normal pastern length, tendon looseness due to prolonged rest, sickness and dietary imbalance.
See **Figures 14** and **127**

Falling pasterns
See Pasterns, down in

Slanting or **Sloping pasterns** The so-called 'slanting pasterns' or 'sloping pasterns' are the most commonly required pastern type in the breed standards, i.e., the happy anatomical mean between 'upright pasterns' on the one hand and 'down in pasterns' on the other.

Slope of pasterns The angle formed by the pastern's longitudinal axis with the horizontal of the ground. Although the actual ideal pastern slope tends to vary with the breed, about 20° to 25° from the perpendicular is considered correct in most instances. Many terms are employed by the breed standards to define the ideal for a given breed, including upright, perpendicular, gentle slope, steep, etc. Such nomenclature, unfortunately, tends to be confusing. It is sufficient to say that, for normal function, some degree of pastern slope is essential.
See **Figure 14**

Steep pasterns
See Upright pasterns

Sunken pasterns Used in the Schnauzer breed standard as a synonym for 'down in pastern'.

Upright pasterns syn. steep pasterns. Pasterns in which the longitudinal axis approaches the perpendicular. The opposite to being 'down in pasterns', upright pasterns are inadequate shock absorbers. Dogs so affected tire more easily and have a slightly shorter stride than those with nor-

Fig. 257b Upright pasterns

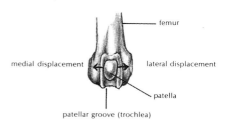

medial displacement

lateral displacement

femur

patella

patellar groove (trochlea)

Fig. 258 Patellar displacement

mally sloping pasterns. Some breeds, e.g., Harrier and Foxhound, are required to have a rather more upright position of pasterns than that usually desired **(Figure 257b)**.
See **Figure 14**

PASTERNS, REAR syn. metatarsus. That section between the hock joint above and the foot below. Often incorrectly termed the 'hock'. Occasionally referred to as hind pastern or back pastern.
See Hindquarters and **Figures 15** and **188**

PATELLA syn. kneecap. A component of the stifle joint.
See **Figure 181**

Patellar dislocation, luxation or **subluxation** An abnormality of the stifle or knee joint leading to dislocation, partial or complete, of the kneecap (patella). Under normal circumstances the kneecap is located in a groove (trochlea) at the lower end of the thigh bone (femur). It is retained in this position by raised trochlear lips on either side as well as by a series of strong, elastic ligaments. Occasionally, when one or other of the trochlear lips is insufficiently well-developed, the kneecap will leave its normal position and come to lie on either the inside of the inner lip (i.e., medial dislocation), or on the outside of the outer lip (i.e., lateral dislocation). Cases of permanent kneecap displacement are referred to as patellar luxation or patellar dislocation. Those in which dislocation is only partial and/or temporary are termed patellar subluxation or 'slippage'. When one leg only is affected the condition is known as unilateral; when present in both, it is referred to as bilateral. Little doubt exists that patellar luxation is due to factors of inheritance. It is seen much more commonly in some Toy breeds, e.g., Chihuahua, Miniature Pinscher, etc., than in the larger breeds. Surgery offers the best chance of permanent correction; other methods of treatment are relatively ineffective **(Figure 258)**.

PATCHY TONGUE
See Tongue

PAUNCHY ABDOMEN
See Abdomen, paunchy

PAW
See Feet Anatomy

PEAK A noun with several meanings, namely: (a) layman's terms for the rather prominent occipital crest of some breeds, e.g., Basset Hound (b) the peculiar coat pattern about the head of some breeds, e.g., Irish Water Spaniel (c) head markings of some breeds, e.g., Welsh Corgi, sometimes referred to as 'widow's peak' **(Figure 259)**.
See Occiput, **Figures 79** and **249**

Fig. 259 Peak: Irish Water Spaniel

PELVIC ANGLE
See Hindquarters

PELVIC GIRDLE syn. pelvis.
See Hindquarters

PELVIS syn. pelvic girdle, hip bone.
See Hindquarters

PENCILLED
See Coat Types: Pily coat

PENCILLINGS; PENCIL MARKS Black lines running along the top of the toes of some breeds, e.g., English Toy Terrier, Gordon Setter **(Figure 260)**.

Fig. 260 Pencilling

PENDENT EARS; PENDULOUS EARS
See Ear Types

PEPPERING The admixture of white and black-banded hairs, i.e., white with black and black with white, which, in association with some entirely black and some entirely white hairs, give rise to the typically grey or pepper-and-salt coloration of the Schnauzer breeds, etc.

PHILTRUM The junction line of left and right upper lip and nostril halves.
See Lips, Naso-labial line, Nose

PI-DOG A crossbred, mongrel type of dog, especially one of Eastern origin.

PIEBALD syn. pinto. Adapted from horse terminology and applied to dogs with irregular black body patches superimposed upon a white background. Ideally the patches should be well-defined and symmetrically placed, covering the head and more than one-third of the body. Known as 'pinto' in America, e.g., Akita breed standard (A.K.C.) **(Figure 261)**.

Fig. 261 Piebald colour pattern: Akita

PIED Common terminology for parti-coloured, unevenly patched hounds. Three types of pied coloration are recognised; (a) lemon pied: spots or patches of mixed lemon, cream or black hairs superimposed upon a white or cream background, (b) hare pied: similar to lemon pied except that the colour patches consist of an orange, khaki, grey and black admixture, giving a hare-like impression, (c) badger pied: again similar to lemon pied, but with a mixture of black, grey and cream hairs in patches, resembling Donegal tweed in appearance **(Figure 262)**.

PIG EYES
See Eye Types

PIG JAW
See Bite: undershot

Fig. 262 Pied colour pattern: Basset Hound

PIGEON CHEST or BREAST Defective chest development due to a breastbone shorter than ideal and characterised by relative absence of prosternum when viewed from the side and accentuated tuck-up into the abdominal floor, commencing only a short distance behind the elbow. Pigeon chest construction is indicative of endurance lack, owing to restrictions upon heart and lung room **(Figure 263)**.

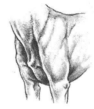

Fig. 263 Pigeon breast

PIGEON TOES; PIGEON-TOED Applied to front feet and toes which turn inwards towards the centre line, both when moving and standing still.
See **Figure 142**

PIGEON-TOED FRONT
See Front Types, **Figure 142**

PIGMENT Used as a noun or adjective (i.e., pigmented) in reference to depth, intensity and extent of colour or markings. For example, German Shepherd Dogs with dark body colour, dark toenails and dark eyes are referred to as being 'well-pigmented'.

PILE Dense undercoat.

PILY COAT
See Coat Types

PINCER BITE
See Bite

PINCHED FRONT
See Front Types

PINK NOSE
See Nose Types

PINTO
See Piebald

PIPE-STOPPER TAIL
See Tail Types

PIP-HEAD A derogatory term applied to specimens with rounded, apple-shaped type skulls, usually coupled with protruding eyes and snipy foreface construction.

PIPS An alternative name for the spots above the eyes of most black-and-tan breeds, e.g., Dobermann, Rottweiler, Gordon Setter. In the Basenji breed the tan spots above the eyes of the black-and-tan variety are known more specifically as 'melon pips' **(Figure 264)**.

Fig. 264 Melon pips: Basenji

PLAIT; PLAITING
See Gait

PLANES, HEAD
See Head planes

PLUME; PLUMED TAIL
See Tail Types

POINT A hunting term to describe the 'freeze' or 'hold' position adopted by gundogs when a game bird has been discovered, to indicate its position to the sportsman **(Figure 265)**.

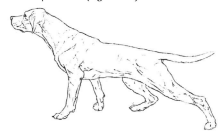

Fig. 265 Point: Pointer

POINT OF THE ELBOW
See Forequarters

POINT OF THE HOCK
See Hindquarters, Calcaneus

POINT OF THE SHOULDER
See Forequarters

POINTS Restricted areas of colour on the face, eyebrows, ears, legs, feet, etc. For example, a Dobermann, by definition, is a black dog with tan points. Used also in reference to specific parts of a dog's anatomy or the hallmarks of a given breed, e.g., 'dishface' of a Pointer, 'spread' of a Bulldog, 'spectacles' of a Keeshond **(Figure 266)**.

Fig. 266 Points: bi-colour: Dobermann

POLL Used in A.K.C.'s breed standard of the Wire Fox Terrier, referring to the top of the head.

POMPOM The round tuft of hair at the end of a Poodle's or Lowchen's tail, produced by trimming. In American usage this word is spelt 'pompon'.
See **Figure 267**

POODLE CLIPS As far as show ring regulations are concerned, all varieties of Poodle may be exhibited in only three varieties of clip, i.e., Puppy clip (permissible for Poodles under twelve months of age), English Saddle (Lion) clip or Continental clip **(Figure 267)**.

POSTERIOR Adjective meaning placed behind, or at the back of; the opposite to anterior.

POT-HOOK TAIL
See Tail Types

POUCH Specialist term for the fold of loose skin overhanging the point of hock; frequently seen in Basset Hounds, etc. **(Figure 268)**.

Continental clip

English lion or saddle clip

Puppy or lamb clip

Kerry clip

Dutch clip

Sporting clip

Fig. 267 Poodle clips

Fig. 268 Pouch

POWDER PUFF A colloquialism to describe the profusely-haired specimens in the Chinese Crested Dog.

PRANCE A gait suggestive of a prancing horse, i.e., springy, bouncing type of movement, emanating primarily from the hindquarters.

PREMOLARS
See Dentition

PREPOTENCY Unusually strong ability to transmit parental qualities to offspring. Mainly said of male dogs rather than bitches. Prepotency in any one area is related to genetic dᵥominance for these characteristics, i.e., homozygocity.

PRICK EARS
See Ear Types

PRIMARY TEETH syn. deciduous teeth or milk teeth.
See Dentition

PROGRESSIVE RETINAL ATROPHY Commonly referred to as P.R.A., progressive retinal atrophy is an inherited form of blindness which, in the dog, occurs in two forms, generalised and central. By way of explanation, the retina is the light-sensitive membrane at the back of the eyeball. Atrophy infers degeneration. Hence P.R.A. leads to gradual loss of retinal sensitivity, impaired function and progressive loss of vision.

Early symptoms include poor sight, especially at dusk or dawn, widely dilated pupils that fail to contract normally when exposed to a light source and eventually total blindness. Although all kinds of dogs, including crossbreds, may develop P.R.A. (also known as 'night blindness'), the condition occurs most commonly in Cairn Terriers, Miniature Long-haired Dachshunds, Elkhounds, Miniature and Toy Poodles, Irish Setters, Cocker Spaniels, Tibetan Terriers and Cardigan Welsh Corgis. No effective method of treatment exists. However, curtailment and/or eventual elimination of the disease is possible by careful selection of blood lines used for breeding.
See Eye Anatomy

PROMINENT EYES
See Eye Types

PROMINENT ORBITAL MUSCLES
See Orbital muscles, Prominent

PROP; PROPPED STANCE A stance, not infrequently adopted as a form of defiance, in which the fore legs come to be extended further out than normal, i.e., appear propped, so that the fore arms, when viewed side on, are not perpen-

Fig. 269 Propped stance

dicular to the ground. Seen from the front, the fore legs may remain vertical to the ground or stand propped out to the side. In order to retain overall balance while propping, the usual position of the hind legs is frequently altered also **(Figure 269)**.

PROPELLER EARS
See Ear Types

PROSTERNUM That portion of the breast bone that projects beyond the point of the shoulder when seen in profile, e.g., Dachshund.
See **Figures 11, 193** and **288**

PROTRUDING EYES
See Eye Types

PUFFS The circular bands of hair left on the forelegs of Poodles prepared in the English Saddle or Continental clip.
See **Figure 267**

PURE-BRED A dog whose parents are of the same breed and who are themselves from parents of the same breed, and so on.

PUTTY NOSE
See Nose Types

Q

QUARTERS Taken from 'quarter, one of the four parts, including a leg, into which the carcasses of quadrupeds are commonly divided'. In the canine species, the word 'quarters' is usually applied to the upper portion only, i.e., pelvic and thigh regions, of the hindquarters, e.g., 'body lighter towards the quarters' (Flat-coated Retriever). However, some breed standards, e.g., Shetland Sheepdog, use the term 'quarters' to include the whole hindquarter section. The addition of the words 'fore' or 'hind' to the word 'quarters' automatically infers the whole section, including the legs.

QUARTERS, BACK A term often used in A.K.C. breed standards to mean hindquarters.

QUARTERS, MUSCULAR or **STRONG** A reference to well-developed, powerfully muscled hindquarters, especially in the rump, croup and upper thigh regions, e.g., 'muscular galloping quarters' (Bedlington Terrier).

R

RACY; RACINESS In general terms a reference to refined, streamlined and elegant appearance, resembling a thoroughbred horse in construction, e.g., Irish Setter. The opposite to cobby or stocky **(Figure 270)**. More specifically, 'racy' may also be applied to individual body regions, e.g., 'racy hindquarters' (Border Terrier), meaning light. Not to be confused with 'weedy' or 'rangy'.

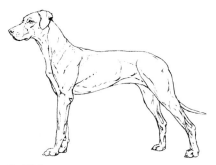

Fig. 271 Rangy appearance

Fig. 270 Racy appearance

RADIUS A bony component of the forearm.
See Forequarters

RAM'S HEAD
See Head Types

RANGY Tall, long in body, often lightly-framed and high on leg; normally used in a derogatory sense **(Figure 271)**.
See **Figures 62** and **270**

RAT TAIL
See Tail Types

REACH A reference to the distance covered with each stride, i.e., a dog said to have plenty of reach or lots of reach is one with maximal stride length.

REACHY NECK
See Neck

REAR PASTERNS
See Pasterns, rear

REAR VIEWS Hindquarters construction is one of the most important considerations in evaluating a dog's qualities. It is the hindquarters region, after all, that supplies most of an animal's propelling power, the forequarters section acting mainly as a stabilising influence. Hindquarters development and structure are analysed from two aspects: side and rear, the former to evaluate thigh muscle mass, angulation, rear pastern slope, etc., the latter to judge bony alignment, inner thigh muscle mass, position of feet and hocks, etc. **Figure 272** depicts the desired norms and the most common variations.

RECEDING CHIN or **LOWER JAW**
See Jaw, receding

REVERSE SCISSORS BITE
See Bite

RIBS The series of flat, narrow, elongated bones forming the chest wall **(Figure 273a)**.
See Chest Anatomy

Back ribs A term often used in A.K.C. breed standards for the rear section of the rib cage.

Barrel or **Barrel-shaped ribs** syn. barrel chest. A chest of rounded contours with ribs beginning to arch soon after emergence from their attachment to the vertebral column. Typical of the British Bulldog, yet listed as a fault in numerous other breeds, e.g., Schnauzer **(Figure 273a)**.
See Chest Capacity

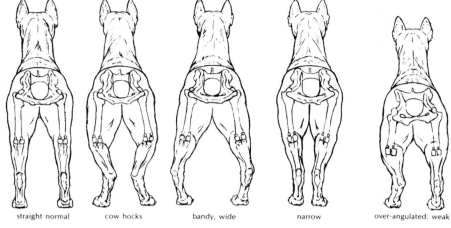

straight normal   cow hocks   bandy, wide   narrow   over-angulated: weak

Fig. 272 Rear views

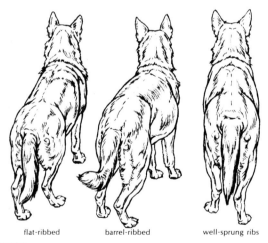

flat-ribbed   barrel-ribbed   well-sprung ribs

Fig. 273a Rib cage construction

Deep in ribs Another way of describing great depth of chest.
See Chest, deep in

False ribs
See Chest Anatomy

Flat ribs The opposite to barrel-shaped ribs. A requirement of the Bearded Collie, but not to be confused with a narrow, slab-sided rib cage, which is considered a fault in most breeds **(Figure 273a)**.
See Chest capacity and Ribs, spring of

Floating ribs
See Chest anatomy

Ribs carried well back syn. ribbed well back, ribbed-up well, well ribbed back, well ribbed-up. A reference to a long rib cage, especially when compared with the length of coupling **(Figure 273b)**.

Slab-sided or **Narrow ribs**
See Flat ribs

Spring of ribs A reference to the shape of ribs after their emergence from their articulation with

Fig. 273b Ribs carried well back

the thoracic vertebrae. Spring of rib has direct influence upon chest capacity. The more pronounced the arch (within reason), the greater becomes exercise tolerance; the flatter the spring or arch, the greater the restrictions on lung and heart development and consequently, the less the anticipated stamina. A dog with correct rib curvature and development is said to be 'well-sprung', 'well-rounded' or 'well-arched' in rib. *See* Chest anatomy, Chest capacity

True ribs
See Chest anatomy

Well-arched ribs
See Ribs, spring of

Well-rounded ribs
See Ribs, spring of

RIB CAGE syn. chest, thoracic cage, thorax. That portion of the canine body encircled by the ribs. *See* **Figure 54**

RIBBED-UP
See Ribs, carried well back

RIDGE Coat pattern, usually relatively long and narrow, formed by hair growing in an opposite direction to that of the surrounding area. Whilst ridges and their associates (whirls, whorls and cowlicks) can and do occur on any part of the body, they are seen most frequently about the head, the sides of the neck and shoulder regions. Undoubtedly the best known example of a 'ridge' in the canine species is that found in the Rhodesian Ridgeback. A genetic phenomenon, this ridge, accompanied by a distinctly shaped whorl on each side, forming the so-called 'crowns', is situated on the back, starting from just behind the shoulders and continuing to the hip bones. It is the hallmark of the breed **(Figure 274)**.
See **Figure 71**

RING STERN; RING or RINGED TAIL
See Tail Types

ROACH or ROACHED BACK
See Back Types

ROAN A colour, likened to 'silvering' in rodents, created by a relatively uniform mixture of coloured and white hairs. For example, black and

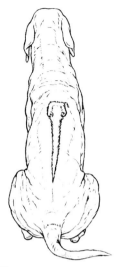

Fig. 274 Ridge

white mixed gives rise to 'blue roan', whereas red and white mixed results in 'red or orange roan'. Dark roan is an even mixture of dark and light hairs; in light roan the dark hairs are fewer and white hairs dominate.

ROLL Employed to describe (a) a fold of skin placed across the top of the nose, e.g., Pekingese **(Figure 275)** and (b) the peculiar and individualistic gait or action of the Pekingese, caused by the relative roundness of this breed's rib cage, coupled with rather short and bowed forearms. *See* Wrinkle

Fig. 275 Roll: Pekingese

ROLLING GAIT
See Gait

ROMAN NOSE
See Nose Types

ROOF OF MOUTH
See Palate

ROOT The base of the tail.

ROPY TAIL
See Tail Types

ROSE EARS
See Ear Types

ROSETTES Small tan patches on each side of the chest above the front legs of basically black dogs, e.g., Dobermann, Manchester Terrier **(Figure 276)**. Also refers to the two patches of hair over the loins of a Poodle trimmed in a Continental clip **(Figure 277)**.

Fig. 276 Rosettes: Dobermann

Fig. 277 Rosettes or bracelets: Poodle

ROUND EYES
See Eye Types

ROUND FEET
See Feet Types

ROUND NECK
See Neck Types

ROUND-TIPPED EARS
See Ear Types

ROYAL COLLAR
See Collar, royal

RUDDER A synonym for tail, mainly in reference to water dogs that use their tails to 'steer' with.

RUFF A collar of profuse, stand-offish, rather long and often coarsely textured hair about the neck.

Typical of such breeds as Schipperke, Chow Chow, Norwegian Elkhound. The term ruff, or neck ruff, includes the whole neck area, i.e., mane, frill and upper part of apron, in contrast to mane, which consists of hair arising only from the top ridge.
See **Figure 191**

RUMP The contours of the combined muscle groups covering the upper surface of the pelvic region. At the front, the rump begins at the end of the loins. At the rear, it blends into the croup and buttocks area. Mostly required to be heavily muscled and convex in appearance, many adjectives, e.g., flat, sloping, steep, etc., are used in the breed standards to describe the various types of rump which may be found in individuals or breeds. They relate to the angle formed by the pelvic girdle and the horizontal line of the spinal column. Most are self-explanatory. Although many standards use the term rump and/or croup interchangeably, the croup is technically the posterior and lower area of the rump, i.e., just above the tail base insertion or set-on of tail **(Figure 278)**.
See Hindquarters

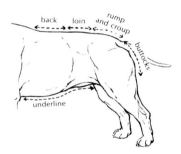

Fig. 278 Nomenclature of body and hindquarter regions

Goose rump Excessively steep pelvic slope (in relation to the horizontal position of the spinal column), often accentuated by lack of muscle development. The opposite to a flat pelvis or rump. Usually associated with a badly set-on tail.
See **Figure 70**

RUNT; RUNTY syn. weed, weedy. Meaning small, spindly, stunted or weak specimens. Mainly applied to puppies or young stock, e.g., 'runt of the litter'.

RUSSET GOLD The individual reddish-brown colour demanded in the Hungarian Vizsla standard.

S

SABLE A coat colour pattern produced by black-tipped hairs overlaid upon a background of silver, gold, grey, fawn, buff, tan or brown basic coat colour in a definite pattern, ranging from the very dark grey-sables (syn. wolf-sable) to the gold or silver sables, with an infinite variety of shades in between, depending on the amount of black-shaded areas involved or depth of colour. The undercoat is usually light and in some breeds and/or individuals there is a black mask. Sable colouring of varying density occurs in many breeds. Typical examples include German Shepherd Dog, Belgian Tervueren, Keeshond and Norwegian Elkhound **(Figure 279)**.
See **Figures 61** and **65**

Fig. 280 Saddle marked colour pattern: Beagle

Fig. 279 Sable colour pattern: German Shepherd Dog

SABRE TAIL
See Tail Types

SACRUM
See Spinal column

SADDLE; SADDLE MARKINGS A noun with three basic meanings for dog fanciers, namely: (a) the 'true' back, i.e., that section of the topline supported by the thoracic vertebrae of the spine (b) colour markings, often black, on and over the back region, similar to, but not as extensive as a blanket, and typical of many hound breeds **(Figure 280)** (c) the rather unusual short hair pattern along the back of mature Afghan Hounds **(Figure 281)**.

SADDLE BACK
See Back Types

Fig. 281 Saddle coat pattern: Afghan Hound

SAGITTAL CREST The ridge of bone at the junction of the two parietal bones. Situated on the outer surface of the cranium, it runs lengthwise to and ends near the base of the skull, where it forms the occipital protuberance.

SAGITTAL SUTURE The fusion of the frontal bones in the centre of the skull, underlying the median line or furrow; mentioned in the Mastiff breed standard.
See **Figure 291**

SAMOYED 'SMILE' The specific expression of this breed, brought about primarily by the combination of black lip margins which turn up slightly at the corners of the mouth **(Figure 282)**.

Fig. 282 Samoyed 'smile'

SAUCY EXPRESSION
See Expression

SAW-HORSE STANCE A stance in which the longitudinal axes of the forearms and/or rear pasterns are not vertical to the ground when viewed from all angles **(Figure 283a)**
See Prop

Fig. 283a Saw-horse stance

SCALP Occasionally employed in place of 'skin covering on skull', e.g., 'scalp should be free from wrinkles' (Airedale Terrier, A.K.C.).

SCAPULA syn. shoulder blade.
See Forequarters

SCIMITAR TAIL
See Tail Types

SCISSORS BITE
See Bite

SCLERA The white membrane surrounding the cornea of the eye. It is this membrane which is referred to in the breed standards when com-

ments such as 'no white to show' or 'ringed eyes a fault' are made.
See **Figure 109**

SCRAMBLED MOUTH
See Mouth

SCREW TAIL
See Tail Types

SCROTUM syn. scrotal sac. The membraneous pouch, located on the abdominal floor, between the hind legs, and containing the two testicles.

SECOND THIGH
See Thigh

SECTORIAL TEETH syn. carnassial teeth.
See Dentition

SELF-COLOURED; SELF-COLOUR syn. whole colour, solid coloured. Of one colour all over, with or without lighter or darker shadings of the same colour.

SELF-COLOURED NOSE
See Nose Types

SELF-MARKED A whole-coloured dog with white or pale markings on chest, feet and tail tip.

SEMI-DROP EARS
See Ear Types

SEMI-HARE FEET
See Feet Types

SET-ON A term applied to (a) the junction of skull and ear lobe and (b) the junction of tail butt and rump.
See Ears, set on

SHAGGINESS; SHAGGY Rough, rugged and hairy coat properties, imparting the ragged outward appearance typified by the Cairn Terrier **(Figure 283b)**.

Fig. 283b Shaggy appearance: Cairn Terrier

SHALLOW IN CHEST
See Chest

SHANK; SHANKS The thigh region. Used in some American breed standards, e.g., Miniature Pinscher, where 'upper shanks' is used for 'upper thighs' and 'lower shanks' in place of 'lower thighs'.
See Thigh

SHARK MOUTH An overshot bite.
See Bite, overshot

SHARP-TIPPED EARS
See Ear Types

SHAWL The part-mane, part-ruff of the Tibetan Spaniel.
See Mane, Ruff

SHELLY; SHELL-LIKE Applied to body development, especially chest dimensions, as well as to leg bone. For example, a shelly body or chest, as mentioned under faults in the Basenji breed standard, refers to chest measurements inadequate in relation to width and/or depth for normal exercise requirements. Shelly bone, on the other hand, is a reference to porous, thin bone, lacking the required strength **(Figure 284,** *see* **Figure 279** for comparison)**.

Fig. 284 Shelly appearance

SHOCK-HEADED Adapted from shock, 'a coarse, tangled mass of hair', and used in the Shih-Tzu breed standard to describe the head hair pattern of this breed **(Figure 353)**

SHORT BACK
See Back Types

SHOULDER In general terms, a reference to the top section of the fore leg, extending from the withers above to the elbow, including the upper arm. The true shoulder region's bony component is the shoulder blade (scapula). This is attached to the chest wall by a series of ligaments, tendons and muscles. On the outside it is covered by muscles and skin **(Figure 285b)**.
See Forequarters, Angulation, **Figures 9, 10** and **11**

SHOULDER ANGULATION
See Angulation, Forequarters

SHOULDER BLADE
See Forequarters

SHOULDER HEIGHT
See Height, Measurements

SHOULDER JOINT A joint in the forequarters formed by the articulation of the shoulder blade and arm, usually alluded to as the 'point of the shoulder', i.e., the area from which angulation of shoulder to upper arm is assessed. The make and shape of the shoulder joint components, plus the lay of the shoulder blade, determine the extent of forward reach **(Figure 285a)**.
See **Figure 137**

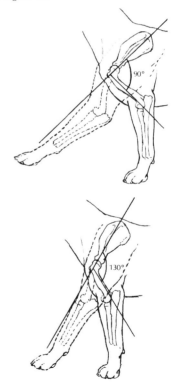

Fig. 285a Shoulder placement and angulation in relation to length of stride

Fig. 285b Shoulder region

SHOULDER, LAY OF
See Angulation, Forequarters

SHOULDER, SLOPE OF
See Angulation, Forequarters

SHOULDER TYPES

Bossy shoulders
See Loaded shoulders

Coarse shoulders
See Loaded shoulders

High in shoulders
See Withers, high in

Loaded shoulders syn. bossy shoulders, coarse shoulders, lumpy shoulders. Normally taken as excessive development of the muscles on the outside surface of the shoulder blades. A dog so affected tends to appear lumpy, over-developed, bossy, bulging or loaded in the forequarters region; it also exhibits a somewhat abrupt base of neck and shoulders junction **(Figure 286)**.

Although shoulder muscle development, from adequate to heavy, is an essential requirement of harness and draught dogs, over-development in that area is likely to lead to restricted, muscle-bound type of movement. A similar appearance can be produced also by a heavier than normal muscle build-up on the underneath surfaces of the shoulder blades.

Fig. 286 Loaded or bossy shoulders

Loose shoulders syn. looseness of shoulders. Shoulder blades insufficiently firm in their attachment to the sides of the rib cage. Animals so affected tend to 'weave' in front when moving;

when standing they often appear to be 'loose in elbow'.
See Weaving

Low at shoulders syn. flat withers, low in withers. Withers set lower than the rest of the backline. A rather unusual physical construction typical of, for example, the Dandie Dinmont Terrier **(Figure 287)**.

Fig. 287 Low in shoulder

Lumpy shoulders
See Loaded shoulders

Not prominent shoulders Used in some breed standards, e.g., Bichon Frisé, to describe a set of shoulder blades sufficiently well covered with muscle on their outer surfaces as well as over the withers region to hide all bony prominences and yet not appear bulging.

Oblique or **Obliquely placed shoulders** syn. slanting shoulders, sloping shoulders, well-angulated shoulders, well laid back shoulders. A reference to shoulder blades, the longitudinal axes of which form an angle of approximately 45° with the horizontal and which, in consequence thereof, angulate at around 90° with their respective upper arms **(Figure 288)**.
See Angulation, **Figure 14,** Forequarters

Fig. 288 Wide, obliquely-placed shoulders and prominent prosternum

Slanting or **Sloping shoulders**
See Oblique shoulders

Steep in shoulders syn. straight in shoulders, upright in shoulders. Indicative of steep angulation, i.e., a scapula/humerus angle in excess of that desired. An animal so affected takes on a somewhat short-necked appearance, due to shoulder blade encroachment into the base of the neck region. Upright shoulders also shorten the length of the forequarters stride. Hence, excessively steep shoulders are considered undesirable in most breeds. There are, however, some exceptions to this rule, e.g., Japanese Chin **(Figure 289)**. See **Figure 14**

Straight in shoulders
See Steep in shoulders

Fig. 289 Steep, narrow shoulders and flat prosternum

Tied-in shoulders Anatomical construction that results in a firmer or more inelastic shoulder blade to chest wall connection than is ideal. Such a defect severely restricts freedom of movement and length of forequarters stride.

Upright shoulders
See Steep in shoulders

Well-angulated shoulders
See Oblique shoulders

Well laid back shoulders
See Oblique shoulders

SHOWING HAW
See Haw

SHOWING TEETH; SHOWING TONGUE A not uncommon defect in some breeds, especially brachycephalic (short-faced) types, e.g., Griffon Bruxellois, British Bulldog, etc., in which a number of teeth are visible when the mouth is shut **(Figure 290)**.
See **Figure 352**

Fig. 290 Showing teeth

SHUFFLING ACTION or **GAIT**
See Action

SICKLE-HOCKED; SICKLE HOCKS
See Hocks

SICKLE TAIL
See Tail Types

SIDE-WINDING syn. crabbing (A.K.C.).
See Crabbing

SILVER EYE
See Eye Colour

SINEW
See Tendon

SINEWY Used to describe lean, hard condition, free of excessive muscle or fat. For example, in the Irish Setter breed standard, 'forelegs straight and sinewy' means clean, non-bumpy structure with tendons at the rear clearly visible.

SINGLE COAT
See Coat

SINGLE TRACKING
See Gait

SKELETON
See Anatomy, skeletal

SKEWBALD Adapted from horse terminology, meaning irregular body patches of any colour other than black, superimposed upon a white ground. Not commonly used in describing dogs, where pied or bi-colour is preferred.
See **Figure 36**

SKULL The bony components of the head. A most complex and highly specialised region, the skull (including the lower jaw or mandible) is divided into two sections: (a) the brain case (*cavum cranii*), formed by the fusion of fourteen individual bones, and (b) the facial and palatal portion (foreface) consisting of thirty-six highly specialised bones, of which all but two (vomer and basihyoid) are paired **(Figure 291a)**. The term skull is often used by dog fanciers in reference to the brain case; this is technically incorrect. The skull as such includes the brain case as well as the facial/palatine segment of the foreface. Furthermore, the terms 'skull' and 'head' frequently appear to be considered one. Evidence of such confusion exists in the wording of many breed standards which deal with both under the same heading and in the same paragraph. Again, such treatment is incorrect. The skull is the head's bony framework and not the head as such. The words 'backskull' or 'topskull' are used in numerous A.K.C. breed standards in reference to the brain case, i.e., the area behind the foreface, e.g., Collie (backskull), Giant Schnauzer (topskull).

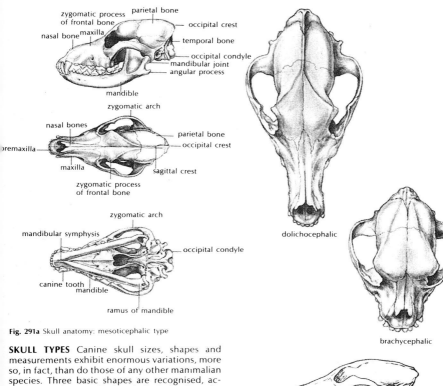

Fig. 291a Skull anatomy: mesoticephalic type

SKULL TYPES

Canine skull sizes, shapes and measurements exhibit enormous variations, more so, in fact, than do those of any other mammalian species. Three basic shapes are recognised, according to the so-called cephalic index formula, i.e., base width in relation to skull length **(Figure 291b)**: (a) dolichocephalic, i.e., a narrow skull base, coupled with great length, breed examples including Borzoi and Collie (b) mesaticephalic, i.e., medium proportions of base width to overall skull length, e.g., Samoyed and Spaniel types and (c) brachycephalic, i.e., broad skull base and short length, typified by the Pekingese and Pug. Apart from the above classification, based on anatomical principles, many varieties and types are referred to in the breed standards. The most important of these are·listed below.
See **Figures 172, 176** and **177**

Apple skull
See Domed skull, Rounded skull

Arched skull An arched skull is one that arches either from side to side or lengthwise from stop to occiput, as opposed to a domed skull, which arches in all directions **(Figure 292)**.

Brachycephalic skull
See Skull Types

brachycephalic

dolichocephalic

brachycephalic

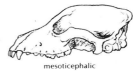

mesoticephalic

Fig. 291b Skull types

Fig. 292 Arched skull: English Setter

Broad in skull A reference to width (not necessarily excessive) between the ears, especially as compared to skull length, e.g., the Golden Retriever breed standard states, 'skull broad' **(Figure 293)**.

Fig. 294 Domed skull: Cocker Spaniel (American)

Fig. 295 Flat skull: Pointer

Fig. 293 Broad rounded skull: Münsterländer

Cone-shaped or **Conical skull**
See Head Types: Cone-shaped

Coarse skull
See Thick in skull

Dolichocephalic skull
See Skull Types

Domed skull syn. apple skull. A brain case roof shaped like an inverted hemisphere, i.e., rounded or arched in all directions and in varying degrees. Breeds with this type of skull include Münsterlander ('slightly domed'), Pyrenean Mountain Dog ('somewhat domed effect'), King Charles Spaniel ('well-domed'). In the Chihuahua it is at its most extreme: such cases are referred to as 'apple skull' or 'apple head' **(Figure 294)**.

Flat skull In contrast to a domed, oval or rounded skull, this type is flat in both directions, i.e., across from ear to ear, as well as from stop to occiput; seen in breeds such as the Australian Terrier, Pointer, Bearded Collie, Clumber Spaniel, etc. **(Figure 295)**.
See **Figure 177**

Mesaticephalic skull
See Skull Types

Oval skull A reference to gentle, curved contours of skull from ear to ear, e.g., English Setter breed standard.

Receding skull One with diverging planes. Mentioned as a serious fault in the Collie and Shetland Sheepdog breed standards.
See Head planes, **Figure 180**

Rounded skull A brain case or topskull curved or arched in both directions, from stop to occiput and from ear to ear, but not as exaggerated as in a domed skull. The degree of arching varies with the breed, e.g., Japanese Chin, French Bulldog **(Figure 296)**.

Fig. 296 Rounded skull

Thick or **Thick in skull** syn. coarse skull. A reference to excessive skull width, especially around the cheek area, due to thick, coarse bone.

Wedge-shaped skull syn. tapering skull.
See Head Types: Wedge-shaped skull

Slab-sided syn. flat-chested, flat-ribbed, flat-sided. The vast majority of breed standards demand a rib shape somewhere between oval and gently rounded when seen in cross-section. It is this shape of chest that determines maximum lung/heart development in concert with freedom and soundness of movement. A dog with ribs flatter (i.e., less curved) than desirable may be termed slab-sided. Such an anatomical construction is almost always considered faulty, e.g., German Shepherd Dog breed standard.
See Chest Capacity, **Figure 273a**

Slack back
See Back Types

SLIPPAGE An unusual term, used in the American Cocker Spaniel breed standard, in reference to patellar luxation or subluxation.
See Patellar luxation

SLOPE OF PELVIS
See Hindquarters

SLOPE OF SHOULDERS
See Forequarters, Angulation

SLOPING BACK
See Back Types

SLOPING SHOULDERS
See Shoulders, Types of

SMOOTH COAT
See Coat Types

SMUDGE NOSE
See Nose Types

SMUT; SMUTTY The encroachment or infiltration of tan coloration into the blue coat areas of the Australian Silky Terrier and the Australian Terrier. An undesirable feature in both breeds, the standards of which require such colour patterns to be distinct. 'Smut' in the British Bulldog means a whole colour with a black mask or muzzle.

SNAPPED TAIL
See Tail Types

SNATCH OF HOCK syn. thrust of hocks.
See Hocks, snatch of

SNIP That portion of a blaze or stripe that deviates into the nostril area.

SNIPY; SNIPINESS Used mainly in reference to a weak or pointed foreface in breeds where such construction is considered undesirable.
See Foreface, snipy, Muzzle, snipy

SNOW NOSE
See Nose Types

SNOWSHOE FEET
See Feet Types

SOCKS White markings on coloured animals, involving the feet and pasterns up to the wrist in front, and/or the feet and rear pasterns up to the hocks behind. Similar markings which extend higher into the forearm and/or lower thigh regions are referred to as 'stockings' **(Figure 297)**.

white stockings   white socks

Fig. 297 Stockings and socks

SOFT BACK syn. hollow back.
See Back Types

SOFT MOUTH
See Mouth

SOFT PALATE
See Palate, soft

SOLID COLOUR or **COLOURED**
See Self-coloured

SOMBRE EXPRESSION
See Expression: Sombre expression

SOUND BONE
See Bone

SOUNDNESS A reference to construction, both physical and mental, that enables a dog to carry out those duties for which it was originally designed. A sound dog, by definition, is one not only physically capable of work, but also one possessing the willingness to perform it. Defining anatomical soundness is a relatively simple task. Gauging an animal's mental aptitude in the show ring is another matter entirely: working and/or obedience tests may be necessary to establish it satisfactorily.

SPECKLE; SPECKLING An alternative to the term 'flecking' or 'ticking' employed in many breed standards. When used for the 'red speckle' variety of the Australian Cattle Dog, it consists of red colour patches, spots and/or dots distributed over a red roan background. Also used in place of flecked or ticked in numerous European breed standard translations to describe the coat colour of several Hound and Gundog breeds, e.g., Grand Bleu de Gascogne, Levesque, Bourbonnais and Burgos Pointers, etc. **(Figure 298)**. See **Figure 133** and Flecking

Fig. 298 Speckled or mottled coloration: Australian Cattle Dog

SPECTACLES Primarily applied to the circular, light-coloured area around the eyes in the basically dark-shaded head of the Keeshond. A characteristic of the breed **(Figure 299)**.

Fig. 299 Spectacles: Keeshond

SPINAL COLUMN syn. spine, vertebral column. Commencing at the neck and running in an unbroken line ending at the tail, the spinal column consists of a series of small bones or vertebrae **(Figure 300)**. With the exception of the three fused sacral vertebrae, these are constructed so as to permit smooth movement between neighbouring bones, cushioned by soft, plate-like intervertebral discs of cartilage, and located between individual sets of vertebrae. The spinal column is divided into five anatomical sections.

(a) Cervical vertebrae: numbering seven, they make up the neck region. The first two, the atlas and axis, differ drastically from the remaining five, their design being highly specialised to allow for almost complete freedom of head movement in all directions **(Figure 301)**. (b) Thoracic vertebrae: thirteen in number, these form the upper or dorsal components of the chest or thorax, and provide anchorage points for the ribs. (c) Lumbar vertebrae: seven in all, these form the upper part of the loin area or coupling. Their function is to act as a support both for and to the abdominal muscles. (d) Sacrum: The sacral region consists of three fused vertebrae; with no movement possible between them, the sacral vertebrae provide an area of firm attachment for the bones and muscles of the pelvic girdle. (e) Coccygeal or caudal vertebrae: gradually reducing in size from the sacral junction to the tail tip; these form the tail. Except for the coccygeal or tail segment, the number of vertebrae in each anatomical section is constant, irrespective of breed.

SPINE
See Spinal Column

SPIRALLY CURLED or **TWISTED TAIL**
See Tail Types

SPLASH An irregularly shaped white mark anywhere on the body, e.g., the Newfoundland breed standard states that 'a splash of white on chest or toes is not objectionable'.

SPLASHED The presence of irregular, usually small white markings on a coloured background or vice versa, e.g., A.K.C.'s Alaskan Malamute breed standard states, 'broken colour extending over body in spots or uneven splashings is undesirable; one should distinguish between mantled dogs or splash-coated dogs', and the Chihuahua breed standard says 'any colour, solid, marked or splashed' (A.K.C.).

SPLASHED TONGUE
See Tongue, patchy

SPLASHES The name given to Boston Terriers with pied brindle spots on a white ground: not a desirable form of colouring in this breed.

SPLAY FEET
See Feet Types

SPOT Usually a reference to the chestnut-coloured mark on the skull of the King Charles Spaniel (sometimes also known as the 'kissing spot'). Ideally situated in the centre skull position and surrounded by a clear, white blaze, the spot should have an approximate diameter of 2 cm (0.8 in). It is also a characteristic feature of many Bleu de Gascogne hounds. Occasionally the term

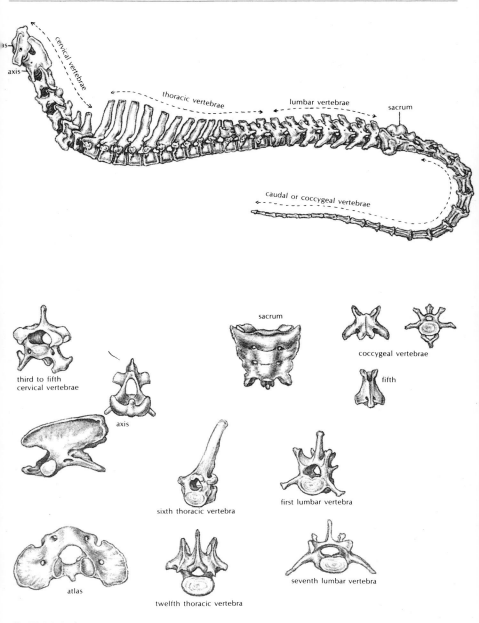

Fig. 300 Spinal column

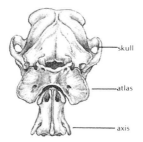

Fig. 301 Articulation of skull, atlas and axis

'spot' is employed to describe a distinct patch of colour on other parts of the body, e.g., the tan spots on the chest of the Gordon Setter, or small white spot on the chest.
See Lozenge mark, Beauty spot, **Figures 34** and **212**

SPOTTED syn. speckled, flecked, ticked.

SPOTTED NOSE
See Nose Types

SPREAD A Bulldog specialist term referring to the somewhat accentuated width of chest as seen between the fore legs when the dog is placed in a show stance **(Figure 302)**.

Fig. 302 Spread: British Bulldog

SPRING OF RIB
See Rib

SPRINGY ACTION or **GAIT**
See Action

SQUARE; SQUARE BODY Basically an animal in which the measurement from withers to ground equals that from point of shoulder to rearmost projection of upper thigh, e.g., many Terrier breeds. Some breed standards, however, employ different definitions, e.g., in the Griffon Bruxellois, squareness of appearance is defined as equal distance from withers to ground compared with that from withers to tail root, whereas in actual fact the dog is longer than it is high. Hence it is important, when discussing square appearance in dogs, to define the points from which such measurements are to be taken **(Figure 303)**.

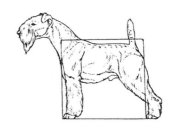

Fig. 303 Square body proportions

SQUIRREL TAIL
See Tail Types

STAMINA
See Endurance

STANCE As in 'show stance'. The posture or position into which a dog is placed to display it to its best advantage.

STANCE, PROPPED
See Prop

STAND LIKE A CLEVERLY MADE HUNTER
See Hunter, Stand like a cleverly made

STAND-OFF COAT
See Coat Types

STAR A small white mark on the forehead **(Figure 304)**.
See Blaze

STATION A reference to height at withers as compared to leg length from point of elbow to ground. A dog is said to be 'of high station' if the length of leg, especially in the forearm section, is appreciably greater than the distance from withers to elbow. Conversely, an animal in which the measurement of withers to elbow greatly exceeds that from elbow to ground level is termed to be 'of low station'.
See **Figure 211**

STEEP An adjective frequently used in relation to angulation, e.g., steep shoulders, steep upper arm, to denote insufficiently acute or wide angles of articulation.

Fig. 304 Star

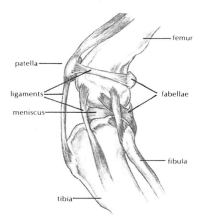

Fig. 305 Stifle joint in profile

STEEP FRONT
See Front Types

STEEP IN SHOULDERS
See Shoulders, steep In

STERN syn. tail. Used in some breed standards, e.g., British Bulldog, English Springer Spaniel, Border Terrier (A.K.C.) and Foxhound.

STERNEBRAE Bony components of the sternum or breastbone.
See Chest anatomy

STERNUM syn. breastbone, brisket.
See Chest anatomy

STIFLE syn. knee joint, stifle joint. A joint in the hind leg, formed by the articulation of upper and lower thighs **(Figure 305)**. The canine stifle joint is an area of special importance to dog fanciers in that 'hindquarter angulation', often mentioned in breed standards, relates directly to the angle formed at this joint, determining such angulation or turn. This ranges from 'good' or 'well-turned' in most breeds, e.g., German Shepherd Dog, to 'moderate' in others, e.g., Hungarian Vizsla. Only a few standards request anatomically 'inadequate' stifle angulation, e.g., Chow Chow; animals so constructed are often referred to as being 'straight in stifle'.
See Hindquarters, Angulation, **Figure 15**

Angulation of stifle
See Stifle, Angulation

Rugged stifle A synonym for strong stifles, clearly demarcated, e.g., English Setter.

Straight in stifle
See Stifle

Well-turned stifle
See Stifle

STILTED Used in the context of 'stilted gait'.
See Gait

STOCKINGS An area of white covering most of the leg, in contrast to 'socks', which cover only the foot and/or pastern.
See **Figure 297**

STOMACH Used in the Elkhound breed standard, i.e., 'stomach very little drawn up', in lieu of the more common 'belly'.

STOP A depression or step down in the topline of the head, situated almost centrally between the eyes, at the junction of the frontal bones of the skull with those of the upper jaw (maxilla) nose (nasal bones) in front. Its shape, depth, width and extent vary according to the structure of the surrounding bones plus the size and position of the frontal sinuses. The stop is most marked in shortfaced types, e.g., British Bulldog, Pekingese; at the other extreme, it is almost undetectable in breeds such as the Collie and Borzoi **(Figure 306)**.
See **Figure 149**

STOPPER PAD The fleshy cushion on the front legs situated at the back of the wrist (carpus); actually the protective covering around the accessory bone. Its main purpose is to act in a shock-absorbing capacity when making contact with the ground during extended gait, e.g., gallop. The stopper pad may also come into operation when negotiating steep rocky terrain.
See **Figure 125**

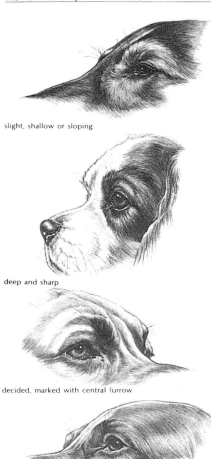

slight, shallow or sloping

deep and sharp

decided, marked with central furrow

average or smooth

flat or imperceptible

Fig. 306 Stop types

STRADDLE; STRADDLING A stance similar in some respects to a saw-horse position, in which both fore and hind limbs are extended both away and out from the body's centre line when viewed from any direction **(Figure 307)**.

STRAIGHT BACK
See Back Types

STRAIGHT FRONT
See Front Types

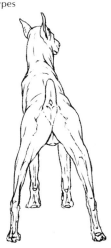

Fig. 307 Straddle

STRAIGHT HOCKS or **HOCKED**
See Hocks

STRAIGHT IN SHOULDER
See Shoulder

STRAIGHT IN STIFLE
See Stifle

STRIPE
See Blaze

STRONG IN COUPLING; STRONGLY COUPLED
See Coupling

STRONG QUARTERS
See Quarters

STUFFY NECK
See Neck Types

STUMPY TAIL
See Tail Types

SUBLUXATION Partial, incomplete or slight dislocation. Not infrequently used to describe cases of temporary patellar dislocation. Also associated with displacement of the hip joint.
See Patellar luxation, Hip dysplasia

SUBSTANCE syn. timber. Used in reference to bone, particularly leg bone, i.e., a dog with heavy substance is one well-developed in bone size, strength and density as related to overall structure and strength. The A.K.C.'s Great Dane breed standard, for example, defines substance as 'that sufficiency of bone and muscle which rounds out a balance with the frame'.

SUPERCILIARY ARCHES or **RIDGES** That region of the frontal bones in the skull forming the brows above the eyes.
See Brows

SWAMPY BACK
See Back Types

SWAN NECK
See Neck Types

SWAY BACK syn. hollow back.
See Back Types

SWEEP
See Swirl

SWINE MOUTH
See Bite

SWIRL syn. hook, sweep. The slight upward turn of the tail in some breeds, e.g., Collie, Pyrenean Mountain Dog. Also known as a hook (Briard) or sweep (Shetland Sheepdog).
See **Figures 322** and **325**

SWORD TAIL
See Tail Types

SYMMETRY; SYMMETRICAL APPEARANCE Used by dog experts in reference to balance and anatomical construction. A symmetrically constructed dog is one in which all parts are balanced harmoniously as regards proportions, shape, size and structure.
See Balance

T

TAIL syn. stern, twist. The tail is the final portion of the spine. Composed of caudal or coccygeal vertebrae, it commences at the root (syn. tail head, base, butt) where it joins the sacral region near the end of the croup. The junction of tail butt to croup is known as the set-on or insertion. A tail set on at a level with the topline, i.e., without a marked drop of croup, e.g., Dobermann, is referred to as 'set on high'; one arising from a sloping croup and/or from a point lower than the topline is termed 'low-set', e.g., Cocker Spaniel.
See **Figure 70**

TAIL BASE or **BUTT**
See Tail

TAIL CARRIAGE The manner of tail deportment; it can be gay, dropped, horizontal, etc., according to the requirements of individual breed standards.
See Tail Types

TAIL FEATHER
See Feather

TAIL ROOT
See Tail

TAIL TYPES The names and descriptions given to the various kinds of tails seen amongst members of the canine race are incredibly varied. The most common are described below.

Bee sting tail Specific terminology for the Pointer, i.e., a tail relatively short, strong, straight and tapering to a point.
See Horizontal tail

Bob or **Bobbed tail** A dog born tailless or a tail artificially docked close to its insertion, e.g., Welsh Corgi Pembroke, Old English Sheepdog, Schipperke **(Figure 308)**.

Fig. 308 Bob or stump tail: Schipperke

Brush or **Brushed tail** A tail covered in medium length bushy, stand-offish and brush-like coat, e.g., Siberian Husky. The hair on such a tail is of approximately the same length on the top, bottom and sides, giving the impression of a round brush **(Figure 309)**.

Fig. 309 Fox-brush tail with sickle curve: Siberian Husky

Carrot-shaped tail Almost self-explanatory: a relatively short tail, strong, thick at the root, tapering to the tip and carried straight up, e.g., Scottish Terrier **(Figure 310)**.

Fig. 310 Carrot tail: Scottish Terrier

Clipped tail
See Docked tail

Cocked-up tail Used in the Cocker Spaniel breed standard to describe a tail raised up at right angles to the backline, in Terrier fashion, instead of being carried level with or below the level of the backline.
See Flagpole tail

Corkscrew tail
See Spirally curled tail, Spirally twisted tail

Crank tail syn. crook tail. A tail carriage in which the root at first is arched out, then hangs down vertically, with the end angled out, resembling an old-fashioned crank or pump handle, e.g., Staffordshire Bull Terrier **(Figure 311)**.

Fig. 311 Crank or pump handle: American Staffordshire Terrier

Crook tail Apart from being a synonym for a crank tail, the term crook tail is sometimes also applied to a malformed tail.

Curled tail Occurs in two basic varieties: single and double curl over the back, with many variations. Examples include: single tight curl over the back only (Lhasa Apso, Elkhound) **(Figure 312)**, single curl falling over the loin with tip pointing towards the thigh (Finnish Spitz) **(Figure 313)**, curled on back to one side (Samoyed) **(Figure 314)**, curled over back with fall of long hair down side (Lhasa Apso) **(Figure 315)**, single or double curl (Basenji) **(Figure 316)**, double curl over hip (Pug) **(Figure 317)**.

Fig. 315 Curled over back with fall down side and kink at end: Lhasa Apso

Fig. 316 Double curl on spine, close to thigh: Basenji

Fig. 312 Tightly curled on back but not on side: Elkhound

Fig. 317 Double curl over hip: Pug

Fig. 313 Falling over loin: Finnish Spitz

Fig. 318 Docked: Norfolk

Fig. 314 Curled on back to one side: Samoyed

Fig. 319 Flagpole: Beagle

Docked tail syn. clipped tail. A tail from which a portion has been removed, usually by surgical means, at four to five days of age. Examples of docked breeds include Boxers, Dobermanns, Poodles and most Terrier varieties **(Figure 318)**.

Double curled tail
See Curled tail

Flagpole tail A long tail, carried erect and straight upwards at right angles to the backline. Similar to a cocked tail, but longer **(Figure 319)**.

Flat tail Specific to the Chihuahua, in which the breed standard states, 'preferred furry, flattish in appearance, broadening slightly in the centre and tapering to a point' **(Figure 320)**.

Fig. 320 Flat tail: Chihuahua

Fox-brush tail
See Brush tail

Gay or **Gaily carried tail** By simple definition, a 'gay tail' is one carried above the horizontal line of the back. However, the actual application of this term varies in interpretation with individual breeds. It is normal carriage in many breeds, e.g., Fox Terrier **(Figure 321)**, in others it is a requirement while working, e.g., Beagle. In some breeds, e.g., German Shepherd Dog, a 'gay tail', standing or working, is considered a fault.
See **Figure 319**

Fig. 321 Gaily carried tail: Fox Terrier

Gnarled tail A badly twisted, malformed tail with joints enlarged, knotted or fused; listed as a fault in the Boston Terrier breed standard.

Hook tail One that hangs down with an upward hook or swirl at the tip, e.g., Briard **(Figure 322)**, Pyrenean Mountain Dog **(Figure 325)**.
See Pot-hook tail

Fig. 322 Upward hook or swirl at tip: Briard

Fig. 323 Horizontal or whip: Bull Terrier

Horizontal tail syn. whip tail, and similar to a bee sting tail, typified by the Bull Terrier **(Figure 323)**.

Kink or **Kinked tail** One that is sharply bent, acutely angled or broken somewhere along its length. Kinked tails may be due to the presence of foreshortened tendons on one side, forcing the tail sideways, or to actual vertebral deformity caused by inherited factors and/or accidental injury. In some breeds, e.g., Lhasa Apso, a kink near the tip of the tail is a normal feature, also in the French Bulldog **(Figure 324)**.
See **Figure 315**

Fig. 324 Kink tail: French Bulldog

Lashing tail A specific description of the active and powerfully moving tail of the Pointer.

Low-set tail
See Tail

Making the wheel Characteristic tail carriage of the Pyrenean Mountain Dog when excited. In repose, the tail of this breed is carried low, with the tip turned slightly to one side. When interested it is raised, and when fully alerted it is curled high above the back in a circle. This action of circle formation is referred to as 'making the wheel' **(Figure 325)**.

Fig. 327 Plumed: Pomeranian

making a wheel

upward swirl
at end
(in repose)

Fig. 325 Making a wheel: Pyrenean Mountain Dog

Merry tail Used by Cocker Spaniel fanciers in reference to this breed's constantly wagging tail; an indication of correct temperament.

Otter tail A strong tail, thick at the base and tapering towards the tip, densely coated with thick, short fur; flat on the underside, rounded in section and specifically constructed to act as a rudder whilst swimming. A requirement for the Labrador Retriever **(Figure 326)**.

Fig. 328 Squirrel tail with plume: Pekingese

Plume or **Plumed tail** Either a tuft of long hairs in the shape of a plume on the tail of some breeds, e.g., Chinese Crested Dog, covering part of the tail only or involving the entire tail, or carried 'plumed' over the back, e.g., Pomeranian and Pekingese **(Figures 327 and 328)**.
See **Figure 344**

Pot-hook tail syn. pot-handle tail. A tail carried up and over the back, raised high above the backline in an arc, never touching nor lying flat against it. Mentioned as a fault in the Lhasa Apso breed standard, in contrast to the Shih Tzu, in which such is considered normal carriage **(Figure 329)**.

Fig. 326 Otter tail: Labrador Retriever

Fig. 329 Pot-hook tail: Shih Tzu

Pipe stopper tail A very short, upright tail; listed as a fault in the A.K.C.'s Fox Terrier breed standard.

Rat tail One that has a thick root covered in soft curls, the lower section being only sparsely coated or entirely devoid of hair, e.g., Irish Water Spaniel **(Figure 330)**.

Fig. 330 Rat-tail: Irish Water Spaniel

Fig. 331 Ring tail

Fig. 332 Ring at end: Afghan Hound

Ring or **Ringed tail** Usually an allusion to a long tail, all or part of which curves in circular fashion **(Figure 331)**; a normal form of tail carriage in some breeds, e.g., Afghan Hound **(Figure 332)**, but considered as faulty in others, e.g., German Shepherd Dog.

Ropy tail An unusual description of a tail, normally well-feathered, but more or less devoid of hair, thus looking gnarled.

Round foxbrush tail
See Brush tail

Sabre tail A tail carried either upwards or downwards in a gently or slightly curved fashion, e.g., Basset Hound and German Shepherd Dog **(Figure 333)**.

Fig. 333 Sabre tail: German Shepherd Dog

Fig. 334 Scimitar tail: Dandie Dinmont Terrier

Fig. 335 Scimitar tail: Gordon Setter

Scimitar tail Similar in all respects to a sabre tail, but with a more exaggerated curve, e.g., Dandie Dinmont Terrier, English Setter **(Figures 334 and 335)**.

Screw tail A short tail, twisted, kinked and or turned in a spiral fashion, e.g., Boston Terrier **(Figure 336)**.

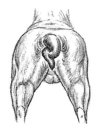

Fig. 336 Screw tail: Boston Terrier

Sickle tail A tail carried over the back in loose, semi-circular fashion, but not snapping flat against the back, e.g., Siberian Husky.
See **Figure 309**

Snap tail Similar in all respects to a sickle tail, but coming into direct contact ('snapping') with the

Fig. 337 Snap tail: Alaskan Malamute

back towards its tip, e.g., Alaskan Malamute **(Figure 337)**.

Spirally curled tail Similar in some respects to a curled or double curled tail, except that it does not curl within itself but rather in a descending spiral, e.g., Wetterhoun **(Figure 338)**.

Fig. 338 Spirally-curled tail: Wetterhoun

Spirally twisted tail A most unusual type of tail, frequently considered as faulty carriage, but typical of the Tazy (Mid-Asiatic Greyhound) in which it is carried low with a spiral longitudinal twist in the end portion **(Figure 339)**.

Fig. 339 Spirally-twisted tail: Tazy

Squirrel tail A long tail that angles forwards sharply, following the line of the back, yet not touching it, e.g., Pekingese **(Figure 340)**. *See* **Figure 328**

Fig. 340 Squirrel tail

Stump or **Stumpy tail** A tail naturally shorter than desirable for a given breed, in contrast to a docked tail. However, such a tail is normal and acceptable in a number of breeds, e.g., Schipperke, Australian Stumpy Tailed Cattle Dog. *See* **Figure 308**

Sword tail One that hangs down without deviation, e.g., Basset Griffon Vendeen. When carried

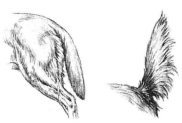

Fig 341a Sword tail carried down: Labrador Retriever
Fig. 341b Tail carried like a sword: Basset Griffon Vendeen

upright, such a tail is synonymous with a flagpole tail **(Figures 341a** and **b)**.

Tapering tail A long, short-coated tail that tapers to a point, e.g., English Toy Terrier **(Figure 342)**.

Fig. 342 Tail with taper to point: English Toy Terrier

Turned over the back tail An exaggerated squirrel or snap type of tail, similar in all respects, but making actual contact along the back. Such a tail is generally plumed, e.g., Pomeranian **(Figure 343)**.

Fig. 343 Tail turned over back: Pomeranian

Tufted tail A long or short tail with a plume of hair at the end, e.g., Chinese Crested Dog **(Figure 344)**, either of natural length or artificially shortened, or trimmed into a pompom, e.g. Poodle **(Figure 345)**.

Twisted tail Some confusion exists between twisted and curled tails. In fact, the only breed standard that mentions the adjective 'twist' in relation to tail carriage is the Tazy. Other kinds of twisted tail are more accurately described under

Fig. 344 Tail with tuft at end: Chinese Crested Dog

Fig. 345 Tufted tail with frou-frou or pompom: Poodle

curled, double curled or spirally curled tails. 'Twist' (the noun) is used as a synonym for 'tail' in some breed standards, e.g., Pug.
See Spirally twisted tail
Whip tail A pointed tail, carried stiffly out in line with the back, e.g., Bull Terrier.
See **Figure 323**

TARSAL BONES
See Hock and Hindquarters

TARSUS
See Hock

TAUT COAT
See Coat

TEETH ANATOMY
See Dentition

TEETH, CRAMPED Irregular, crowded alignment of teeth, either in reference to incisors, due mainly to insufficient width of dental arches, i.e., snipiness, or to premolars and molars in short-faced (brachycephalic) breeds.
See **Figure 75**

TEETH ERUPTION
See Dentition

TEETH TYPES
See Dentition

TEMPLES syn. trumpet. As in man, the area just behind and slightly above the eyes, i.e., the region of the temporal bone, covered by temporal muscle.
See **Figure 291**

TENDON syn. sinew. The bands of rather inelastic fibrous tissues formed at the termination of a muscle, joining or attaching it to a bone. The largest and strongest tendon in the dog is the so-called Achilles tendon in the hind leg. It anchors the thigh muscle groups into the fibula tarsal bone or 'point of the hock'.
See Hindquarters, **Figures 2** and **186**

TERRIER FRONT or **FRONTED** The long-legged Terrier breeds possess forequarters construction which (a) when viewed front on, should be moderately wide only and have forearms that run parallel to one another from chest to ground (i.e., the distance between the elbows and that between the wrists is identical), both the line and strength of the forearms continuing in an unbroken manner right down to the feet without tapering off in the pastern area, and (b) when seen side on, should feature acceptable shoulder joint angulation, with shoulders and arms of approximately equal lengths; also forearms which stand at right angles to the ground, plus relatively short and upright pasterns. The terms 'terrier front' or 'terrier-fronted' are often used to describe front assemblies of similar construction in breeds other than Terriers, whether they are considered either virtues or faults **(Figure 346)**.

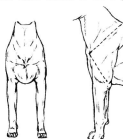

Fig. 346 Terrier front

TESTICLES syn. testes. The male gonads, part of the reproductive system. The testes' two main functions are the production and storage of male sperm cells (spermatozoa) and the secretion of the male sex hormone, testosterone.
See Cryptorchid

THICK SKULL
See Skull Types

THIGH syn. upper thigh, shank. The anatomical region between the hip joint above and the stifle below, i.e., the muscle groups surrounding the thigh bone (femur). Dog fanciers frequently speak of three thigh regions, namely (a) upper thigh, i.e., the area from hip to stifle joint as mentioned above (b) lower thigh (syn. gaskin, second thigh), i.e., the muscular region between stifle

and hock joints, and (c) inner thigh, that portion of the upper thigh muscles located on the inside of the thigh bone (i.e., the vastus and abuctor muscle groups) **(Figure 181)**.
See Hindquarters, **Figures 7, 8** and **307**

INNER THIGH
See Thigh

LOWER THIGH syn. gaskin, second thigh, shank. See Thigh

NARROW THIGH Insufficiently strong muscular development of the thigh regions when viewed in profile **(Figure 347)**.

Fig. 347 Narrow thighs

SECOND THIGH
See Thigh

SLANTING THIGH Used in A.K.C.'s Miniature Schnauzer breed standard, meaning correctly sloping thighs.

WIDE THIGHS A request for maximum development of upper thigh muscles, measured from front to back when viewed in profile **(Figure 348)**.

Fig. 348 Wide thighs

THIGH BONE syn. femur.
See Hindquarters

THIRD EYELID syn. nictitating membrane. A semi-cartilagenous structure located at the eyes'

inner corners, and when required, used as a protective device to shield the eyes from injury, act as a windscreen wiper, etc. With the exception of its rim, the third eyelid is usually of pinkish colour, with the outer edge pigmented to blend with the surrounding palpebral margins or eyelids. On occasions the outer edge remains unpigmented, imparting a quasi-haw-eyed appearance to facial expression, despite the presence of tight lower eye rims. From a judge's viewpoint it is important to differentiate between these two conditions, i.e., uncoloured nictitating membrane and ectropion. The latter, in most breeds, is an undesirable defect, usually of genetic origin. Non-pigmented third eyelids, on the other hand, are rather inconsequential, apart from their effect upon general appearance **(Figure 349)**.
See Haw Eye, **Figure 109**

THORAX
See Chest

THOROUGHBRED APPEARANCE
See Appearance, thoroughbred

THROAT The under portion of the neck, i.e., the opposite side to the crest, especially near the head junction.
See **Figure 11**

THROATINESS; THROATY A reference to loose, pendulous folds of skin under the throat and underside of the neck. Typified by the Basset Hound and Bloodhound, in which such conformation is considered desirable. In contrast, throatiness is mentioned as a fault in numerous breed standards, e.g., Pointer, English Setter.
See **Figure 237**

THROAT LATCH The area of head/neck junction immediately behind/below the lower jaw angles.
See **Figure 11**

THROATY NECK
See Neck Types, Throatiness

THUMB MARKS Spots or marks, usually of black colour, in varying positions on a number of breeds, e.g., (a) immediately above the feet at the front of the pastern region of the Manchester Terrier (b) similarly marked as above, as well as under the chin, in the English Toy Terrier (c) on the forehead of the Pug (syn. diamond) **(Figure 350)**.
See **Figure 78**

TIBIA One of the components of the lower thigh region.
See Hindquarters

TICKED; TICKS Mentioned in many breed standards, especially Hound and Gundog, in relation to very small areas of hair different in colour to

normal third eyelid:
coloured edge

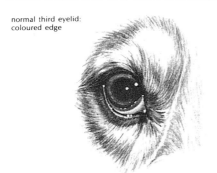

unpigmented third eyelid
colourless edge
palpebral fissure

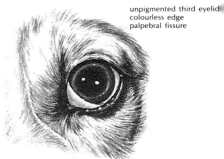

Fig. 349 Third eyelid (nictitating membrane)

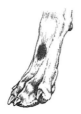

Fig. 350 Thumb mark

an animal's basic ground colour and distributed throughout the coat; usually dark spots on a white ground. Similar or often synonymous to flecks and speckles. Examples include Australian Cattle Dog, Bluetick Coonhound, German Short-haired Pointer, etc.
See **Figures 133** and **298**

TICKING A coat colour pattern.
See Ticked

TIED IN ELBOW
See Elbows, out at

TIED IN SHOULDER
See Shoulder, Types of

TIGHT-FITTING JACKET
See Jacket, tight-fitting

TIGHT-LIPPED JAWS
See Jaws

TIMBER Colloquial expression for bone, usually leg bone.

TOEING-IN
See Gait

TOENAIL syn. claw. A horny extension of the third phalanx of each toe. The toenail, varying in colour from light through brown to black, is

curved and compressed from side to side, forming a beak-like structure. It is well-supplied with blood (as evidenced when a toenail is trimmed too closely) and grows at a rapid rate; so much so that, unless worn down or trimmed periodically, it may grow in a circular fashion, even to the point of penetrating the foot pad. Excessive toenail length can also result in normally well-knit toes spreading or separating from one another, thus allowing easy penetration of stones, etc., between the pads, with consequent lameness or injury **(Figure 351)**.
See Feet Anatomy

Fig. 351 Toenail anatomy

TOES ANATOMY
See Feet Anatomy

TOE TYPES Constructed of a series of small bones called phalanges, the basic shape of canine toes, viewed in profile, is arched. The degree of arching or curvature varies with the individual and/or breed from 'well knuckled-up' or highly arched, i.e., cat foot, through to rather flat and extended, i.e., hare foot. The toes of dogs also tend to differ in their relationship to one another. Toes close up against their partners, forming a cat foot, are referred to as compact, closely knit or close cupped. Conversely, those tending to drift or stand away from each other are termed spread, deviating, open, scattered or loosely knit. The types of toes named in the breed standards are listed below.

Arched toes syn. cat feet.
See Toe Types, Feet Types

Close cupped toes
See Toe Types, Feet Types

Closely knit toes
See Toe Types

Compact toes syn. cat feet.
See Toe Types, Feet Types

Spread toes
See Toe Types

Tightly-knit toes syn. cat feet.
See Toe Types, Feet Types

Well knuckled-up toes syn. cat feet.
See Toe Types, Feet Types

Well padded toes A reference to deeply cushioned toe pads.
See Feet Anatomy

Well split-up toes Used in some breed standards, e.g., Chihuahua and Pug, to describe the clear, distinct and deep separation of individual toes from each other, as compared with the strongly webbed toes of some Arctic and water-retrieving breeds, e.g., Irish Water Spaniel, Chesapeake Bay Retriever, Alaskan Malamute. Occasionally also referred to as 'well split-up feet', e.g., Magyar Agar.

TONGUE, LOLLING An overlong tongue, i.e., one that protrudes from the mouth, usually (but not always) from the space between the lower lateral incisors on one side and the adjacent canine tooth. When not caused by panting, a lolling tongue is an anatomical defect seen not infrequently in brachycephalic (short-faced) breeds, e.g., Pug, Boxer, Pekingese **(Figure 352)**.

Fig. 352 Showing or lolling tongue

TONGUE, PATCHY; TONGUE, SPLASHED An incompletely pigmented tongue in breeds where blue-black coloration is required, e.g., Chow Chow, Shar-Pei; also black spots on an otherwise red tongue, e.g., Australian Terrier. Some individual dogs of any breed have a blue spot on their tongues.

TOPCOAT
See Coat

TOPKNOT syn. tuft. Long, woolly, fluffy or silky hair on top of the head of some breeds, e.g., Afghan Hound, Bedlington Terrier, Shih Tzu **(Figure 353)**.

Fig. 353 Top-knot: Shih Tzu

TOPLINE Normally taken as a dog's entire upper outline seen in profile, starting at the ears and ending at the tail, e.g., 'sloping topline' (German Shepherd Dog, Alaskan Malamute. By that definition 'level topline' is an obviously incorrect and impossible demand of some standards, e.g., Australian Terrier, Papillon, Weimaraner, etc., in which 'topline' and 'backline' have been confused.
See **Figure 31**

TOPSKULL
See Crown, Skull

TORSO syn. body.

TOTTERING
See Action

TRACE The black line along the back of the fawn variety of the Pug, required to extend from the occiput to the tail **(Figure 354)**.

Fig. 354 Trace: Pug

TRIANGULAR EYES
See Eye Types

TRIANGULAR-SHAPED EARS
See Ear Types

TRICHIASIS A rather painful anatomical abnormality, related to entropion and caused by eyelashes erupting in abnormal, misplaced positions and directions. Some eyelashes, occasionally many, grow in towards the eyeball. Constant eyelash-to-eyeball contact results in irritation and, finally, injury. Early symptoms of trichiasis include tear secretion, sensitivity to light as evinced by squinting, etc. Trichiasis is thought by most experts to have an inherited background. It is much more common in some breeds, e.g., Miniature Poodle and Pekingese, than others.
See Entropion, **Figure 106**

TRI-COLOUR A coat of three colours, usually black, white and brown; used primarily in describing Hound breeds **(Figure 355)**.

Fig. 355 Tri-colour: Hamilton Stövare

TROT
See Gait

TROUSERS; TROUSERING Longish hair at the back of both upper and lower thighs of some breeds, e.g., Pyrenean Mountain Dog and Keeshond.
See Breeches, Culottes and **Figure 46a**

TROWEL-SHAPED EARS
See Ear Types

TRUE BITE syn. scissors bite.
See Bite

TRUE FRONT
See Front Types

TRUMPET The canine temple. The slight depression or hollow located on either side of the skull, just behind the orbit (eye socket), e.g., Weimaraner breed standard (A.K.C.).

TUCK-UP syn. cut-up. The appearance produced by the abdomen's underline as it sweeps upwards into the flank and/or hindquarters region. In some breeds, e.g., Whippet and Greyhound,

the tuck-up is relatively sudden, acute and exaggerated by exceptionally deep chest development. In other breeds its presence varies from moderate, e.g., Miniature Pinscher, Dobermann, to barely noticeable, e.g., Sussex Spaniel, Affenpinscher, Rottweiler. Also referred to as 'cut-up', e.g., English Toy Terrier, French Bulldog, Manchester Terrier **(Figure 356)**.

Fig. 356 Tucked-up abdomen or tuck-up

TUFTED TAIL
See Tail Types

TULIP EARS
See Ear Types

TURN OF FOREARM
See Forearm, turn of

TURN-UP syn. upsweep. The bent upward configuration of the lower jaw (mandible) in some brachycephalic (short-faced) breeds, e.g., British Bulldog. The so-called 'repandous (bent upwards) part of the under jaw', mentioned in the Boxer breed standard **(Figure 357)**.
See **Figure 57**

Fig. 357 Turn-up: Boxer

TUSKS syn. canines.
See Dentition

TWIST In some breed standards, e.g., Pug, the word 'twist' is used synonymously with the word 'tail'.

TWISTED TAIL
See Tail Types

U

ULNA
See Forequarters

UMBRELLA Synonymous with veil, but shorter. Referred to in the breed standard of the Hungarian Puli; also applies to the Komondor and Old English Sheepdog, etc., **(Figure 358)**. *See* Veil and **Figure 59**

Fig. 358 Umbrella or curtain: Old English Sheepdog

UNDERCOAT
See Coat

UNDERHUNG syn. undershot.
See Bite

UNDERLINE The combined contours of the brisket and abdominal floor. Known variously as 'underline' (Bull Terrier), 'under body' (Miniature Schnauzer, A.K.C.), 'lower body line' (Pyrenean Mountain Dog), 'abdomen line' (English Springer Spaniel, A.K.C.), etc.
See **Figure 278**

UNDERSHOT
See Bite

UNILATERAL CRYPTORCHID
See Cryptorchid

UNSOUNDNESS The opposite to soundness. A dog is considered unsound if for any reason, physical and/or mental, it is incapable of carrying out the functions for which it was designed.

UN-UNITED or **NON-UNITING ANCONEAL PROCESS** An inherited defect located at the elbow joint. Sometimes referred to as elbow dysplasia, this condition is not uncommon in German Shepherd Dogs, Mastiffs, Basset Hounds and Labrador Retrievers. Symptoms include transient forequarter lameness. Accurate diagnosis is based on X-ray examination. Surgery offers the only successful form of treatment.
See **Figure 105**

UP-CURVE Referring to shape of underline in A.K.C.'s breed standard of the English Springer Spaniel.

UP ON LEG syn. high on leg, of high station.
See Station

UPPER ARM syn. arm.
See Forequarters

UPPER JAW
See Jaw

UPPER THIGH
See Thigh

UPRIGHT EARS
See Ear Types

UPRIGHT PASTERNS
See Pasterns

UPRIGHT SHOULDERS
See Shoulder Types

UNDERLINE The combined contours of the brisket coupled with proud bearing, e.g., Kerry Blue Terrier breed standard.

UPSWEEP
See Turn-up

V

V-SHAPED EARS
See Ear Types

VARMINTY
See Expression, varminty

VEIL syn. curtain. That portion of a dog's forelock hanging straight down over the eyes, and at least partially covering them, e.g., Skye Terrier. Ex-

Fig. 359 Veil: Lhasa Apso

treme veiling, e.g., Lhasa Apso, is synonymous with 'curtain' **(Figure 359)**. The term 'umbrella', on the other hand, refers to a cap-like fall of hair, e.g., Old English Sheepdog, Hungarian Puli, etc. See **Figures 140 and 358**

VENT According to some authorities, the area surrounding the anus; others claim it to be the tan-coloured hair under the tail of some breeds: this definition would include the vulva of bitches as well as the anus.

Vent, barrelled A most unusual description, used in the A.K.C.'s Miniature Pinscher breed standard, for a protruding anal sphincter which, when viewed side on, is similar in appearance to the vent of an eggbound bird.

VENTRAL In anatomy, pertaining to the belly. The opposite to dorsal.

VERTEBRA; VERTEBRAE
See Spinal column

VERTEBRAL COLUMN
See Spinal column

VINE-LEAF EARS
See Ear Types

W

WAIST; WAISTED Normally a clearly defined narrowing of the body over the loins (lumbar region) when compared with width of chest as seen from above, e.g., Miniature Pinscher. Also used in reference to appearance in profile, e.g., Basenji **(Figure 360)**.

Fig. 360 Waist

WALK
See Gait

WALL EYES
See Eye Colour

WEASELNESS Mentioned as an undesirable characteristic in the A.K.C.'s Old English Sheepdog breed standard, weaselness refers to the lean, long and snake-like body of that animal, coupled with rather short legs. Weaselness, in many respects, is the opposite to legginess.

WEAVING
See Gait

WEEDINESS; WEEDY Inadequately boned, lightly framed, stunted in development or unthrifty. 'Weediness' is mentioned as an undesirable defect in numerous breed standards, e.g., Australian Silky Terrier.
See Runty, Coarseness

WELL-ANGULATED
See Angulation

WELL-COUPLED syn. short coupled, strongly coupled.
See Coupling

WELL CUT-UP
See Cut-up

WELL-FILLED OUT UNDERNEATH THE EYES An often-quoted reference to strength of foreface near its point of origin at the muzzle/brain case junction.
See Chiselling, **Figure 52**

WELL-KNIT A reference to body sections firmly joined by strong, well-developed muscles. Often taken as a synonym for 'well or short coupled', i.e., a powerful loin section joining the chest to the hindquarters **(Figure 361)**.

Fig. 361 Well-knit forequarters: British Bulldog

WELL-KNUCKLED-UP TOES syn. cat foot.
See Toe Types, Feet Types

WELL-LAID SHOULDERS syn. well-angulated shoulders.
See Angulation, Forequarters

WELL-PROPORTIONED Another way of describing correct balance between various parts of the body.
See Balance

WELL-SET NECK
See Neck Types

WELL-SPLIT-UP FEET
See Feet Types

WELL-SPLIT-UP TOES
See Toe Types

WELL-SPRUNG RIBS
See Ribs, well sprung

WELL-SUNKEN EYES
See Eye Types

WET NECK
See Neck Types

WHEATEN Fawn, pale-yellow colour, sometimes referred to as straw. Commonly found in a number of Terrier breeds, e.g., Scottish Terrier, Norwich Terrier, Soft-coated Wheaten Terrier, etc.

WHEEL BACK
See Back Types

WHIP TAIL
See Tail Types

WHIRL syn. whorl. A ridge of hair growing in a circular pattern.
See Ridge, **Figures 71** and **274**

WHISKERS The usually harsh, thick and longish hair arising from the chin (chin whiskers), from the sides of the face (moustache), or from a combination of both (beard). The degree, extent, amount and texture of whiskering varies both with the individual and the breed. In the Norfolk and Norwich Terrier, for example, slight whiskering is requested. The Kerry Blue Terrier breed standard, on the other hand, merely asks for whiskers. On an Afghan Hound, the whiskers, when present, tend to be relatively soft; those on the Giant Schnauzer are requested to be both heavy and stubby, etc.
See Beard, Moustache, **Figures 33, 107** and **108**

WHOLE COLOURED
See Self-coloured

WHORL
See Whirl, Ridge

WIDOW'S PEAK Triangularly shaped coat markings on the forehead, commonly seen on sable and bi-coloured dogs, e.g., Welsh Corgi, German Shepherd Dog, Rough Collie, Alaskan Malamute, Saluki, etc. The triangle's base faces the skull, its apex pointing forwards. Also known as 'domino markings' in the Afghan Hound, or 'grizzle' in the Saluki **(Figure 362)**.
See **Figure 79**

WIDE FRONT
See Front Types

WIRE-COATED; WIRE-HAIRED; WIRY-COATED syn. broken coated, bristle coated. Possessing a harsh-textured, crisp and wiry top coat.
See Coat: Broken-coated

WITHERS Anatomically, the region of union between the upper portion of the shoulder blade on the one hand and the spinous processes of the first and second thoracic vertebrae on the other. Topographically, the withers are located just behind the base of the neck at the neck/back junction; a significant area, as a dog's height is measured from this location.
See Forequarters, **Figure 11**

Drop through withers
See Back dropping through withers

Fig. 362 Widow's peak: German Shepherd Dog

Flat or **Flat in withers** syn. low at shoulders, low in withers. Anatomical construction in which the topline, from the base of the neck to the rump, runs in an almost straight, horizontal line. Dogs so affected usually display a clearly, even acutely, demarcated neck/back junction as well as an ill-defined withers region.
See **Figure 22**

High in withers Anatomical construction in which the topline, when viewed in profile, slopes down towards the rear. Typical of, among others, the German Short-haired Pointer, Miniature Pinscher, Spinone Italiano, etc.
See **Figures 28, 189** and **270**

Low in withers Unusual and often faulty anatomical development in which the withers area, viewed in profile, appears lower than the rump region, i.e., a topline sloping up towards the rear. A desirable feature in the Old English Sheepdog, Chesapeake Bay Retriever, etc.
See **Figure 29**

Withers separation An unusual, almost unique, description employed in the A.K.C.'s Samoyed breed standard in relation to the space palpable between the scapula's vertebral borders at the withers region. The distance of separation recommended, i.e., between 2.5 cm and 3.8 cm (1 in to 1.5 in), in the opinion of some experts, is necessary to permit adequate freedom of movement.

WOLF-SABLE
See Sable

WRINKLE; WRINKLING Loose folds of skin on or

about any part of the body and, more commonly, the head. The degree and extent of wrinkling present amongst dogs varies tremendously. It is maximal in the Shar-Pei, where deep and long skin folds envelop the entire animal. Basset Hounds and Bloodhounds also serve as good examples of wrinkling, although in these breeds the folds tend to be restricted more or less to the

Fig. 363 Wrinkling or frown: Basenji

head and neck regions. At the other end of the scale are breeds like the Chow Chow and Basenji. In the latter, wrinkling is restricted to the head region and is obvious only when the dog is alerted. In both breeds the expression produced is referred to as a frown **(Figure 363)**.

WRINKLE, OVERNOSE In the Pekingese, a fold of skin above the nose and midway between the eyes. Variable in length and width, the presence of an overnose wrinkle plays a major part in influencing expression. Sometimes also referred to as a 'roll'.
See **Figure 275**

WRIST Colloquial terminology for 'carpus'. The joint between forearm and pastern on the front legs.
See Forequarters

WRY BITE; WRY MOUTH
See Mouth, wry

X

XIPHOID PROCESS Portion of the breastbone.
See Chest anatomy, **Figure 54**

Z

ZYGOMATIC ARCH The bony ridge forming the lower border of the eye socket (orbit). Composed of two parts, it is an extension of the zygomatic or malar bone at the rear of the skull. The strength and/or prominence of the zygomatic arch is mentioned in numerous breed standards, e.g., Rottweiler, and greatly influences the contours and shape of the face.
See **Figure 291**